THE VIET-MINH REGIME

GOVERNMENT AND ADMINISTRATION

IN THE

DEMOCRATIC REPUBLIC OF VIETNAM

By

Bernard B. Fall
Research Assistant, Southeast Asia Program
Cornell University

Data Paper: Number 14
Southeast Asia Program
Department of Far Eastern Studies
Cornell University, Ithaca, New York

Issued jointly with the
Institute of Pacific Relations

April, 1954

THE INSTITUTE OF PACIFIC RELATIONS

The Institute of Pacific Relations is an unofficial and non-partisan organization, founded in 1925 to facilitate the scientific study of the peoples of the Pacific area. It is composed of autonomous National Councils in the principal countries having important interests in the Pacific area, together with an International Secretariat. It is privately financed by contributions from National Councils, corporations and foundations. It is governed by a Pacific Council composed of members appointed by each of the National Councils.

In addition to the independent activities of its National Councils, the Institute organizes private international conferences every two or three years. Such conferences have been held at Honolulu (1925 and 1927), Kyoto (1929), Shanghai (1931), Banff, Canada (1933), Yosemite Park, California (1936), Virginia Beach, Virginia (1939), Mont Tremblant, Quebec (1942), Hot Springs, Virginia (1945), Stratford, England (1947), and Lucknow, India (1950). The Institute conducts an extensive program of research on the political, economic and social problems of the Pacific area and the Far East. It also publishes the proceedings of its conferences, a quarterly journal, Pacific Affairs, and a large number of scholarly books embodying the results of its studies.

Neither the International Secretariat nor the National Councils of the Institute advocate policies or express opinions on national or international affairs. Responsibility for statements of fact or opinion in Institute publications rests solely with the authors.

NATIONAL COUNCILS

American Institute of Pacific Relations, Inc.
Australian Institute of International Affairs
Canadian Institute of International Affairs
Comite Français d'Etudes des Problemes du Pacifique
Indian Council of World Affairs
Indonesian Institute of World Affairs
Japan Institute of Pacific Studies
Netherlands Council on Pacific Affairs
New Zealand Institute of International Affairs
Pakistan Institute of International Affairs
Philippine Council, Institute of Pacific Relations
Royal Institute of International Affairs

IPR INTERNATIONAL SECRETARIAT --- 1 East 54th Street, New York 22, N. Y.

FOREWORD

The end of the Pacific war marked the beginning in Indochina of the bitter conflict between France and the Democratic Republic of Vietnam which now threatens all of continental Southeast Asia and is an influence in the domestic and external strategies of the governments of all the world's major powers. The background, development, and involved issues of this long-standing struggle are highly disordered and complex. Interested laymen and students have had to try to understand the confused situation in Vietnam on the basis of incomplete information blurred and oversimplified through censorship, propaganda, inadequate news coverage, and the lack of essential documents.

Particularly crucial has been the shortage of basic objective data on the political, administrative, and military organization of the native government of the Democratic Republic of Vietnam. Since September, 1945, this government has won control over half the population of Vietnam or eleven million people; has been able to influence many more outside the several discrete zones under its direct administration; and with little aid from outside until after 1950 has more than successfully withstood all efforts of the French-- in recent years heavily supported by American funds and materiel-- to reestablish their authority over the entire country of Vietnam. The Democratic Republic of Vietnam and its adherents are still commonly called the "Viet-Minh," the popular Vietnamese term for the now disbanded "League for the Independence of Vietnam," which was organized during the war under the aegis of the Indochinese Communist Party, receiving for a time support from the Kuomintang government of China and from the American Army. What little public information there has been on the Viet-Minh regime since its establishment and during its remarkable development under the leadership of Ho Chi Minh has come largely from the propaganda offices of that regime itself or from obviously biased French or Communist sources. Even the excellent recent study by Ellen J. Hammer, The Struggle for Indochina (Stanford: Stanford University Press, 1954), has had to rely heavily on such sources, and particularly those publicly available in France.

In view of this situation, Mr. Bernard Fall, the author of this study, has performed a useful service in gathering and evaluating on the spot in Vietnam materials available only there and in organizing these and other data into this systematic account of the structure and functioning of the government of the Democratic Republic of Vietnam. Mr. Fall is a young French citizen with a background of academic training in political science and practical experience in military government. Having served for more than three years in the French Army, and having worked closely under American Army officers in occupied Western Germany, he came to the United States to carry on post-graduate work in international relations at Syracuse University. Deciding to specialize on Southeast Asia and particularly Indochina, he was able to work in that area from March through November, 1953. This trip, paid for entirely by himself, allowed him to complete in the field research already begun for his doctoral dissertation on the post-war political evolution of Vietnam. His finished dissertation will include a comparative study of both the nationalist Associated State of Vietnam developed by the French since 1948 under the former emperor, Bao Dai, and the Democratic Republic of Vietnam under Ho Chi Minh. The present monograph, accordingly, utilizes only a portion of the materials collected during his sojourn in Indochina.

Aided by his French civil and military status, Mr. Fall was able to obtain excellent cooperation from French and Nationalist Vietnamese administrative and military officials; and he made good use of his unusual opportunity. He was permitted to circulate without restriction, and was given access to and permission to quote from normally classified documents. In the following study, most of his sources of information are documented, although in a few instances exact references cannot be given for reasons of military security or in order not to violate confidences placed in him by officials.

Apart from propaganda documents, official sources of information on the Democratic Republic of Vietnam include the Official Journal published regularly by the government and containing all legislative texts and decrees; but with the exception of the issues printed in Hanoi in 1946, no complete set of this journal is known to exist in a location accessible to western students. However, the more important government texts which the regime wishes to publicize are printed in extenso in Cu'u Quoc ("National Salvation"), the official newspaper of the government which is published in several regional editions for the separate zones into which the Democratic Republic's territory is divided. Many other official texts have fallen into the hands of French Union Forces during combat operations or through the interception of couriers. Finally, because of the distances involved between different zones, many government announcements or administrative orders that require implementation at the regional or local level are transmitted in Morse code over the extensive radio network of the Republic and can thus be regularly intercepted by French or Vietnamese Nationalist monitoring stations. This last source provides the greater part of what is known of the working of the governmental machinery of the Republic. All of the above available sources of information were open to Mr. Fall during his stay in Vietnam.

There remains the problem of interpreting such official sources as those mentioned above, of determining the extent to which government orders are actually put into everyday practice or the extent to which actual behavior and events conform to the often glowing accounts given in official reports. Some check has been provided in recent years by the "auto-criticisms" of officials and others which are made public by the government, following the vogue set by other Communist regimes. Insights into the problems faced by the government of the Democratic Republic and into the realities of life in the zones controlled by that regime may also be obtained directly from people moving across the battle lines; "line-crossing" permits are issued by both the Republican authorities and the Nationalist Vietnam police authorizing the bearer to enter enemy-held territory for "family" or other reasons. Information from such informants as well as from all other available sources are summarized in French intelligence evaluation reports, extracts from which the author has been privileged to see.

Inevitably a good deal of personal judgment and even conjecture must enter at this stage into a study such as that presented in this Data Paper. The nature of the war-- with important ad hoc developments going unrecorded and much documentary evidence being lost-- and the intense bitterness which has been built up among the major protagonists in Vietnam will make difficult if not impossible the writing of any complete or objective account of events during the past decade in that unhappy country. In the meantime, Mr. Fall has produced a work which students of the region will find a helpful addition to their meager store of information.

The staff of the Cornell University Southeast Asia Program wishes to thank the International Secretariat of the Institute of Pacific Relations for aid which has made it possible to issue this Data Paper jointly with the Institute. Neither the Cornell Program nor the Institute assumes responsibility for statements of fact or opinion expressed in this study, for the content of which the author alone is responsible.

Lauriston Sharp, Director
Southeast Asia Program

Department of Far Eastern Studies
Cornell University
Ithaca, New York
April, 1954

ACKNOWLEDGEMENTS

I hereby wish to record my thanks for the help received from many quarters in gathering the material for this study. I am particularly indebted to the Office of the Commissioner-General of the French Republic in Indochina, its Political Advisers and Staff in North and South Vietnam; to the Director of the Vietnam National Security Police in North Vietnam; the Heads and Staff of the Vietnamese and French Liaison-Pacification Bureaus in Hanoi and Saigon; and many officers and men of the Vietnam National Army and the French Union Forces in the Far East for their invaluable aid and assistance during the field research phase of my assignment.

Likewise, I wish to express my appreciation for the documentary material courteously put at my disposal by the Vietnam News Service in Rangoon, Burma, and by other sources close to the Republican Government.

I also owe much to Professor Lauriston Sharp, Director, and to Professor George McT. Kahin, Associate Director of the Cornell University Southeast Asia Program for their critical comments, and particularly for Dr. Sharp's help in editing this text in its final form. Mr. William W. Gage of the Southeast Asia Program kindly checked Vietnamese terms.

My thanks go also to my wife Dorothy for doing most of the art work contained in this study, and to my sister Lisette for doing a considerable amount of research and compilation on the French material used in the text.

Last but not least, I wish to express my gratitude to Mr. William L. Holland, Secretary-General of the International Secretariat, Institute of Pacific Relations, for his kind help and encouragement, given when it was most needed.

In jointly sponsoring the issue of this study, neither the Southeast Asia Program nor the Institute of Pacific Relations assumes responsibility for opinions expressed herein; for such views I am solely responsible.

Bernard B. Fall

Ithaca, New York, April, 1954.

CONTENTS

CONTENTS (cont'd)

CONTENTS (cont'd)

APPENDICES

CHARTS

MAPS

ILLUSTRATION

PART ONE: THE BIRTH OF THE DEMOCRATIC REPUBLIC OF VIETNAM

1. The "Government-in-Exile".

     Ironically enough, the Democratic Republic of Vietnam(D.R.V.N.)or Viet-Nam Dan Chu Cong Hoa which is today called a "Communist satellite," began in 1941 as a private political venture (with economic overtones) of the then Kuomintang warlord of Kwangtung Province, Marshal Chang Fa-kwei. With the progressive weakening of French power in Indochina under Japanese encroachments, Vietnamese revolutionary elements in the autumn of 1940 had staged a series of local uprisings in Vietnam which had been put down promptly by the French. Thereafter various Vietnamese nationalist groups and members of the outlawed Indochinese Communist Party (ICP), or Dong Duong Cong San Dang, began to assemble in China under the protective wing of Chang Fa-kwei and his able aide, General Hsiao Wen (1)*, in order to create a common liberation front against both the French and the Japanese. The Communist elements had regrouped in Kwangsi during the early spring of 1941. There they were reorganized by their old leader Nguyen Ai Quoc who had written more than fifteen years earlier: "All races must unite in one movement of revolt against France, and they shall not fail to institute a revolutionary tribunal to judge that colonial coterie as it deserves to be judged." (2) In May, 1941, the Communists met at Chinghsi (3) in a "congress" together with representatives of several other less important groups: the New Vietnam Party; the Vietnam Revolutionary Youth League; elements of the old Vietnam Nationalist Party, Viet-Nam Quoc Dan Dang, or VNQDD; and various National Salvation-- Cu'u Quoc-- organizations. During the course of this meeting all these groups banded together to create the League for the Independence of Vietnam, or Viet-Nam Doc Lap Dong Minh Hoi, better known as the "Viet-Minh."

     A second conference met under the auspices of the Kuomintang generals at Liu-chou, Kwangsi, on October 4, 1942, which was supposed to achieve the creation of a unified Vietnamese revolutionary committee-- a step which the Chinese thought should properly precede the creation of a Vietnamese "govern-ment-in-exile" on the model of such governments as existed in Europe during that period. All major political factions of Vietnamese nationalism (the VNQDD; the Vietnam Restoration Party, Viet-Nam Phuc Quoc Dang, or "Phuc Quoc"; and nationalist delegates from Vu Khong Khanh's group in Yunnan) were represented with the exception of the ICP, which had been excluded. (4) However, the Viet-Minh was duly represented. (5) Under strong Chinese pressure, a Vietnam Revolutionary League, Viet-Nam Cach Menh Dong Minh Hoi, or "Dong Minh Hoi" (DMH), was launched by the conference on October 10, 1942, dominated by the VNQDD and under the leadership of Nguyen Hai Than, a Vietnamese who had resided in China since 1908 and who held a general's rank in the Kuomintang Army.

     However, that state of union between the Vietnamese political groups was to last but a few months. More and more group leaders balked at the completely ineffectual leadership of Nguyen Hai Than. Nguyen Ai Quoc, along with several other Vietnamese political leaders, was jailed by the Kuomintang for nearly eighteen months in the hope that this would bring about a more harmonious cooperation within the Dong Minh Hoi, but to little avail. Nguyen Ai Quoc was to remain in jail until early 1943, at which date Chang Fa-kwei recognized the failure of the Dong Minh Hoi league as a rival of the Viet-Minh league and

_____

*Footnotes are placed at the end of each Part.

for the time being gave Nguyen Ai Quoc, the man who was now introduced to
Chungking as Ho Chi Minh, a practically free rein in the re-organization of
the Vietnamese nationalist revolutionaries. (6)

Finally, another congress was held at Liu-chou between March 25 and 28,
1944, in the course of which the platform for a "Provisional Republican Government of Vietnam" was hammered out. Although the Viet-Minh's past "lone-wolf"
activities (e.g., the establishment of its own guerilla groups and spy net-
works in Vietnam) were criticized, basic differences were finally patched up
and once again Chang Fa-kwei succeeded in imposing the Chinese viewpoint.
The newly created "government" had a non-Viet-Minh majority. Ho Chi Minh,
however, held a cabinet post in the new combination. The Vietnamese had begun
to climb the thorny path to independent statehood.

The program of the newborn government was brief: a) liquidation of both
the French and the Japanese grip on Vietnam; b) independence for Vietnam with
the help of the Kuomintang. The new government, however, had no armed forces
at its disposal with which to forward its ambitions and most of the nationalist
parties had various reasons for not actively intervening on Vietnamese soil.
Only the ICP possessed the necessary network of agents and bases -- such as
its Nuoc Hai stronghold in Cao Bang Province, established early in 1943 -- to
be able to expand its operations within Vietnam with any chances of success.
It did so now, but under the nationalist Viet-Minh rather than the party
label, and with the blessing of the Provisional Republican Government of
Vietnam which remained based in southern China.

It cannot be denied that the Viet-Minh showed an amount of political
foresight which the other Vietnamese parties were far from sharing. While the
latter counted on the Kuomintang to carry them into power in Indochina, the
Viet-Minh mounted extensive recruiting campaigns and acquired a reputation
of ubiquity throughout the back areas of North Vietnam. They won many recruits,
particularly among the Vietnamese soldiers of disbanded French colonial forces,
who became the hard core of the Viet-Minh's nascent army and who are today
the elite of the military cadres of the DRVN. Furthermore, while the old
nationalist party leaders preferred the comparative safety and comfort of
Yunnan and Kwangsi, Ho Chi Minh was the only cabinet member of the Provisional
Government who volunteered to enter Vietnam in 1944 "in order to intensify
the struggle." Joining up with the partisan groups of Vo Nguyen Giap, a
young Communist history professor who had held out in various North Vietnam
mountain areas since 1942, Ho soon controlled the vital Thai Nguyen area
which, to this day, has remained a major Viet-Minh stronghold.

The complete elimination of the French military forces and political
authority by the Japanese coup de force of March 9, 1945, with the ensuing
total vacuum of any civil administration (for the Japanese merely occupied
the strategic communication lines while leaving the Indochinese countryside
pretty much to itself) proved to be the ideal situation for a successful
development of Viet-Minh control over a considerable area of northern Tongking.
Practically without having fired a shot, the Viet-Minh could boast of having
"liberated" North Vietnam. The activities of the Viet-Minh guerillas were on
a minute scale at best, when compared with other resistance movements in Asia
and Europe which had to face greater handicaps. The only major armed attack
thus far on record is that of 500 Viet-Minh against 40 Japanese gendarmes at
the mountain resort of Tam Dao on July 17, 1945, in the course of which the
Japanese finally lost eight men. (7) In addition to minor engagements, the
Viet-Minh carried out light sabotage and intelligence work.

Being the most active and the only sizeable insurgent group in Indochina during the aftermath of the Japanese coup, Ho Chi Minh's forces naturally received the bulk of the new American weapons and communications equipment as well as other military equipment parachuted into Indochina through the help of the American Office of Strategic Services (O.S.S.). Within a short time during the summer of 1945, and with the additional acquisition of Japanese and French weapons after VJ-Day, Ho Chi Minh possessed the necessary wherewithal to build up a fighting force capable of easily outmatching both the few French troops which had retreated into Yunnan (only to be disarmed there by their Chinese allies), and any rival Vietnamese nationalist groups who might re-enter Vietnam from Kwangsi. The Viet-Minh had won its first battle.

2. The Struggle for Power (1945-46).

It was in the period following the Japanese collapse that the Viet-Minh showed a surprising ability in fighting a three-front diplomatic war against the Chinese, the French and the other Vietnam nationalists without deviating from its basic aims. The Potsdam Conference, among its other undoings, had decided to split Indochina along the 16th parallel into a northern, Chinese-occupied zone, and a southern zone to be occupied by British forces. These allied troops, however, did not arrive in force until September, while French forces were at first excluded. This fact both the "neutral" Japanese and the Viet-Minh interpreted to mean that all French nationals had to remain in the various internment and concentration camps into which they had been put by the Japanese the preceding March. Thus the Viet-Minh, already in a strong position, had almost a month following VJ-Day in which to maneuver freely.

On August 7, 1945, Ho Chi Minh threw off whatever ties he still had with the "Provisional Republican Government" and in a move that curiously resembled what had happened a year before in Poland, established a "Vietnam People's Liberation Committee" of his own, of whose fourteen members all but three happened also to be members of the Indochinese Communist Party or of the Viet-Minh. (8) By August 15, 1945, VJ-Day, this "Committee," the Uy Ban Dan Toi Giai Phong Viet-Nam, controlled nearly all of North Vietnam, with no opposition in sight.

However, the impending arrival of the Kuomintang occupation troops -- and Chinese-supported, rival Vietnamese nationalist leaders would be in their baggage trains -- forced Ho Chi Minh to temporize. The "People's Liberation Committee" was dissolved and a new "Provisional Government of the Democratic Republic of Vietnam" was formed in Hanoi on August 29, 1945. This new Government was politically more representative than the Liberation Committee, but Ho Chi Minh had retained the presidency and the foreign ministry for himself, and had handed the key cabinet posts of interior (police), national defense, finance, propaganda, education and youth to his Party or Viet-Minh stalwarts. Among the non-Communists of this first Government were members of the Indochina branch of the French Socialist Party, one brother-in-law of a French Communist member of parliament, one Catholic, one doctor "known for his extremist opinions," one member of the VNQDD, one jurist, one engineer, and one man-of-letters. (9)

The Viet-Minh had successfully weathered its first battle with its nationalist rivals and their Chinese protectors. They still had to face the French, but that was to be at a later date. One brief interlude occurred with the puppet government supported by the Japanese at Hué, the ancient capital of Vietnam, where Bao Dai, the once French-protected Emperor of Vietnam, had shed French overlordship after the Japanese coup of March 9, 1945, by proclaiming the independence (Doc Lap) of Vietnam, by declaring the protectorate treaty with France null and void, and by eventually organizing a united Vietnam by integrating the old colony of Cochinchina and the protectorates of Annam and Tongking into a single unified state.

On August 25, 1945, Bao Dai abdicated with his government and transmitted his powers to the newly-constituted Provisional Government of the Democratic Republic of Vietnam with the following words:

> ...2) We request the new Government to treat kindly all those parties and groups which have fought for the independence of the country, even though they were not following closely in line with the popular masses. This will give them the opportunity to participate in the reconstruction of the country, and will show that the new regime is built upon the absolute unity of our entire population.

> 3) We invite all groups and parties, all the different classes of people, as well as the Royal Family, to be all united, and to support the Democratic Government wholeheartedly in order to consolidate our national independence...(10)

In a message to the members of his own clan, Bao Dai said:

> ...having declared that I would rather be a common citizen in an independent state than be the king of a subjugated nation, I decided to abdicate in order to hand over the rule to a Government capable of leading the forces of the whole country towards the consolidation of National Independence...(11)

In view of this action the then Provisional Government of the Democratic Republic of Vietnam could proclaim that it was the legitimate successor to the Imperial Government of Vietnam, since the abdication of the Emperor had been voluntary, and the transfer of authority explicit. There can be no doubt that certain pressures had been exercised at Hué, although Bao Dai himself still declared two years later, and in the safe haven of Hong Kong:

> My hand had not been forced: I abdicated of my own free will. If I had wanted to remain /emperor7 a civil war could have resulted. I was given to understand and my government was given to understand that the people did not want the monarchy anymore. I did not want to oppose myself to the natural evolution of the people; mine wanted to become a democracy, and I yielded. (12)

Once again, the Provisional Government under the leadership of Ho Chi Minh was farsighted enough not to let pass the opportunity of sanctifying the regime by reinforcing its nationalist aspect. Ho appointed Bao Dai as "Supreme Adviser" to the Government, a post which the latter accepted under the name of "citizen" Nguyen Vinh Thuy. The Viet-Minh now had scored a double victory: it not only had succeeded in becoming a controlling power holding the governmental apparatus, but also had obtained for its Government all the appurtenances of legality.

One last step remained to complete this impressive list of bloodless political successes: the declaration of independence. It followed hardly one week after Ho Chi Minh had consolidated his internal position, on September 2, 1945, and was carefully designed to appeal sentimentally to the anti-colonialist leanings of the United States, from which Ho expected to receive most of the help he needed. Nowhere in the declaration is there any reference to the achievements of the Soviet Union; on the contrary, the declaration rather refers to the spirit of 1776 and to the French Revolution, as well as to the Teheran and San Francisco Declarations. Here again, Ho's Government acted with a commendable amount of cold realism: the Soviet Union was thousands of miles away and preoccupied with the problems of China and Eastern Europe, while American help was near and perhaps available.

It is apparently at this juncture that certain political errors of judgment were made whose detailed examination does not enter within the purview of this study. The sole reports thus far available on conversations held in Hanoi between members of the Provisional Government and officers of the small United States military group which had just entered the area stem from unofficial French sources (13) and from some sparse American news reports (14). French sources, both Communist and non-Communist, concur in their opinion that these discussions were concerned, among other things, with the granting of economic advantages to the United States or to Americans by the Ho Government in exchange for political and military support, and that these "negotiations" broke down because American demands were excessive. (15) However charmed by Ho's winning personality or prejudiced against French colonialism these O.S.S. and other Americans might be, or whatever claims individuals may have made, it is clear that they were not spokesmen for official American policy, nor is there evidence that they even influenced such policy. Nevertheless, the impression apparently developed among some of the hopeful Ho group and the few highly sensitive and vulnerable French officials in Hanoi, that American military personnel there were speaking for their government in Washington. The French felt that their worst fears of an American post-war grab in Indochina were being corroborated, while Vietnamese of the Provisional Government imagined their independence would be officially championed throughout the world by the United States. Franco-Vietnamese relations were for long strongly influenced by these opposed unrealistic definitions of the situation.

3. The Consolidation of Power.

The first acts of the new Government were directed to gathering a maximum of public following. On August 29, 1945, the Provisional Government abolished the marketing tax which was levied upon all products sold on public markets; on September 7, the individual income tax was done away with; and on September 14, professional taxes were eliminated. While such actions were obviously popular, they put the fledgling Government into a disastrous financial situation. Customs duties, which were to be the mainstay of government revenue, were entirely non-existent since the Kuomintang troops "exported" everything within sight free of customs, and also accommodated the local merchants—for a fee—by exporting their merchandise via Chinese military convoys. Needless to say, all such euphoric measures were soon repealed and often enough replaced by measures more stringent than those existing heretofore (see Part V).

However, another danger arose with the arrival of the Chinese troops. At first, they purely and simply ignored the existence of the Provisional

Government and set about to eliminate systematically all Vietnamese local-administrations on their way to Hanoi and to replace them with "Administrative Committees" composed of members of the VNQDD, the VNPQD or the DMH who had arrived with them. Soon, the Viet-Minh's sphere of authority was practically reduced to Hanoi and the southern part of North Vietnam, and most of North Vietnam assumed the air of a "Little China" with each political faction holding a geographically distinct part of the territory with its own military leaders and armed bands (see Map I).

Again, Ho Chi Minh used the full measure of his political acumen and experience in dealing with the Chinese. (16) By an amazing coincidence, the famous "Gold Week" (second week of September, 1945, during which the population was asked to contribute gold so that arms could be purchased abroad) was held simultaneously with the arrival of the troops of Generals Lu Han and Hsiao Wen. While there is no evidence that great amounts of weapons were purchased abroad, the hitherto hostile attitude of the Kuomintang generals to the Provisional Government changed into one of nearly friendly neutrality, and Ho succeeded in maintaining almost unchallenged control of Hanoi and all its administrative services, including the treasury, as well as the powerful Bach-Mai Hanoi radio transmitter. At the same time, while he acknowledged the fact that his political rivals held most of the valley towns in the north, Ho maintained his control of the thousands of small villages scattered throughout the countryside, and his control of the central communications network gave him a tremendous advantage over his opponents in spreading his propaganda as well as orders throughout all of Vietnam. Ho began to negotiate with the various nationalist groups and arrived at an agreement on October 23, 1945, which was denounced a few days later, on November 2, by Nguyen Hai Than, leader of the Chinese-sponsored DMH, as too favorable for the Viet-Minh. It was then that Ho Chi Minh decided to eliminate temporarily from the public scene the Indochinese Communist Party. During a Party congress held in Hanoi on November 8, 9 and 10, 1945, a decision of the Central Executive Committee of the Party stated that:

> ...so as not to harm National Unity, the members of the Communist Party of Indochina have decided to dissolve the Party.

This measure was seemingly designed to have the double effect of reassuring the Chinese, Southeast Asians, and the West as to the primarily nationalist aims of Ho Chi Minh, and of considerably broadening the base of internal popular support upon which the Viet-Minh had to depend for the time being. A pertinent explanation can be found in a Viet-Minh circular which fell into French hands in 1952, dated November 1, 1951:

> ...the Party policy must be a pliable policy; indeed, no matter how supple we are, if we keep the name of "Communist Party" a certain number of landowners, progressive intellectuals and members of religious sects would not want to follow us...

> At the present time, there are in the world several Labor Parties or Marxist-Leninist parties of the working class which do not carry the name of Communist Party, such as the United Polish Workers' Party, the Hungarian Workers' Party and the Korean Workers' Party.

> Those parties have changed their name for several reasons, some different from ours, some identical with ours, but the aim of those changes of

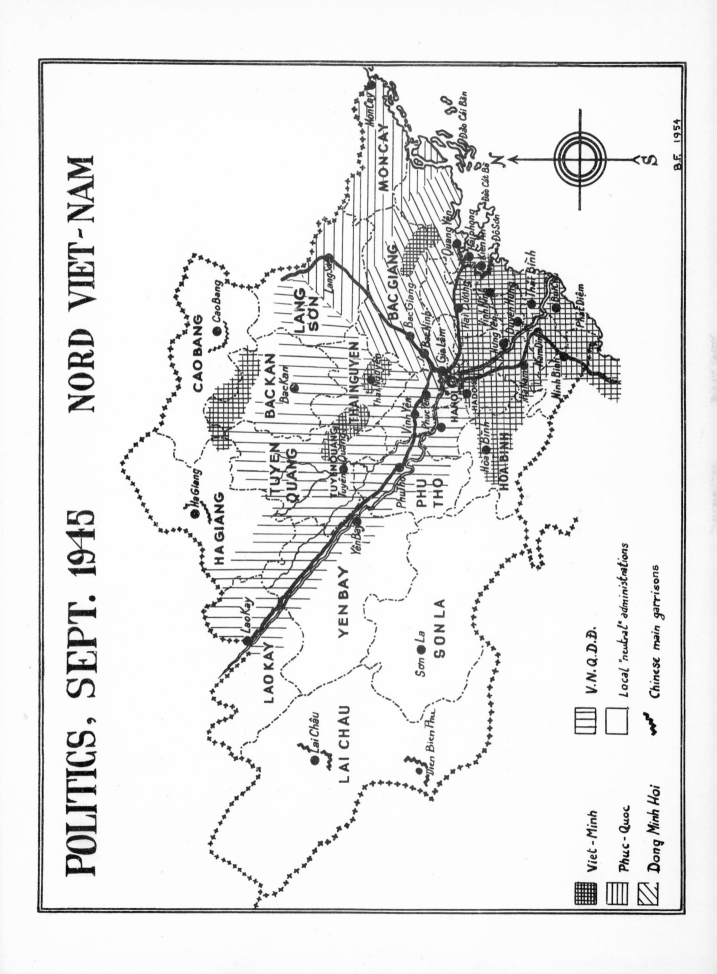

POLITICS, SEPT. 1945   NORD VIET-NAM

B.F. 1954

Legend:

- ▨ Viet-Minh
- ▥ Phuc-Quoc
- ▧ Dong Minh Hoi
- ▥ V.N.Q.D.Đ.
- ☐ Local "neutral" administrations
- ⌇ Chinese main garrisons

Place names / provinces:

CAO BANG — Cao Bang
HA GIANG — Ha Giang
BACKAN — Backan
TUYEN QUANG — Tuyen Quang
LANG SON — Lang Son
THAINGUYEN — Thai Nguyen
BAC GIANG — Bac Giang
MON CAY — Mon Cay
Đảo Cái Bầu
Đảo Cát Bà
Đảo Yen Ah
Đồ Sơn
Quang Yen — Haiphong — Kien An
Bac Ninh
Gia Lam
HANOI — HADONG
Vinh Yen
Phuc Yen
PHU THO — Phu Tho
YEN BAY — Yen Bay
LAO KAY — Lao Kay
LAI CHAU — Lai Châu
Dien Bien Phu
SON LA — Son La
HOA BINH — Hoa Binh
Ninh Binh
Phat Diem
Nam Dinh
Thai Binh
Bui Chu
Hung Yen
Thai Duong
Lang Son

name is always: to unify the working class and the true revolutionary party of the workers, to unite the national and democratic forces against the imperialists and their valets, to consolidate the regime of popular democracy...(17)

Still, the DMH insisted upon the execution of the Liu-Chou agreement of March, 1944, which the Viet-Minh was loath to put into practice. Fighting broke out between the Viet-Minh and armed bands of the VNQDD and DMH, particularly at Vinh Yen and Ha Giang. On September 13, the Provisional Government had promulgated a series of decrees, among which was one which gave their Security Service "...the right to arrest any individual dangerous to the security of the Vietnam Republic..., (18) a blanket authorization, indeed, to eliminate all persons whose political opinions did not parallel those of the regime. There was but little opposition on the part of the Chinese as long as the arrests were limited to the "small fry." However, they stepped in when the government attempted to search the headquarters of the VNQDD's newspaper, Viet-Nam. A new agreement was signed among the warring political factions on November 18, to be broken again on December 8. This time, however, the Viet-Minh succeeded in splitting away a good part of the DMH party from the main body. Slowly, the disintegration of the opposition parties began under the very noses of their sponsors, the Kuomintang "liberators."

4. Constitutional Structure.

On September 8, 1945, Ho Chi Minh signed a decree providing for general suffrage in Vietnam and for the convocation of the first National Assembly following general elections, originally planned for December 23 of the same year. However, in view of the unsettled situation and under pressure of the Chinese-backed nationalist groups which justly felt that they had not been given a fair chance to campaign effectively, Ho signed a new decree on December 18 delaying the elections until January 6, 1946, in order to give "...hesitant men of valor" an opportunity to present their candidacies. This hardly satisfied the DMH and VNQDD who knew that their chances in an open electoral contest would be next to nil, not so much for the generally-advanced reason that the Viet-Minh was overwhelmingly popular as for the fact that the Viet-Minh had had six months during which to implant its power through police, army, and control of communications and that it represented "the Government" to the inexperienced and largely illiterate average Vietnamese voter who, in natural distrust of what he did not know (i.e., the newly-arrived nationalists), would vote for the Viet-Minh, long associated with the appearance of independence.

Therefore, on December 22, 1945, a third agreement was signed between the DMH, the VNQDD and the Viet-Minh (all other splinter parties having more or less fallen by the wayside) which, substantially, stipulated that the nationalist parties would not sabotage the elections; that as of January 1, 1946, two Ministries would be handed over to the two parties; that a to-be-created Vice-Presidential post would be given to Nguyen Hai Than, leader of the DMH; and finally that without participating in the elections the VNQDD would receive fifty and the DMH twenty seats in the future Quoc Hoi or National Assembly. (19) It is quite obvious that the type of elections in which the party in power is able to "deliver" in advance a fixed number of seats to rival parties falls somewhat short of what is currently accepted as democratic parliamentary procedure. The concessions made by Ho were minor indeed. The two cabinet posts which the Viet-Minh relinquished were those of Public Health and National Economy and the Vice-Presidency was quickly so organized that it exercised no influence whatever on affairs of state. Furthermore, Nguyen Hai Than was more than 70 years old and had resided in China for so long that he could hardly express himself adequately in Vietnamese anymore! Lastly, a promise to neutralize the key cabinet posts of Interior and National Defense in the cabinet to be formed after the elections was again successfully circumvented by the Viet-Minh by slowly stripping the Defense Ministry of all powers in favor of the military commander-in-chief; and by transferring the police and security powers of the Minister of Interior to autonomous Security Services.

The elections themselves took place in an atmosphere of excitement and festivity skillfully developed by the propaganda services of the Provisional Government. The results were hardly unexpected. An American account speaks of the "wide popular response" and "enthusiastic support" which Ho's candidates "who stood, often unchallenged," received. (20) Viet-Minh sources speak of an overall election participation of "above 90 percent," with 100 per cent results for Ho Chi Minh in Ho's own constituency and an overall pro-Government vote of 97 per cent in the Hanoi area. (21)

It is interesting to note some local reactions to the elections, especially as reflected in newspapers which were critical of the Viet-Minh for not being sufficiently anti-French. For example, the newspaper Viet-Nam of the VNQDD wrote on December 18, 1945:

> Comrads of the Viet-Minh! Do not be shameless enough to go to the polls. If you are not capable of fighting the French in Cochinchina (22), or of tilling the land so as to nourish your compatriots (23), do not be so shameless as to go to the polls on election day, to put flowers on your houses...so as to become the laughing stock of your compatriots.

After the Viet-Minh had decided to delay the elections until January 6, 1946, the Dong Minh Hoi newspaper Lien Hiep ("Union") on December 20, 1945, carried an article which said:

> The Viet-Minh was forced to delay the elections for fear of public opinion.

> The Viet-Minh intended...to hide itself behind the screen of a so-called National Assembly. Unfortunately for it, a wind of counter-action has swept the country as a whole... Faced with such a reaction of the public, the Viet-Minh used one of its usual tricks: it whipped out a text delaying the elections so as to permit numerous candidates to present themselves...

> Still, we have to watch them because they are definitely capable of holding partial elections in certain areas under the pretext that these provinces could not be notified in time for the delay of the election date to the 6th of January, 1946. The results thus obtained could permit them to succeed in their projects without giving the population an opportunity to control the true general results.

As to the elections themselves, the newspaper Viet-Nam of January 8, 1946, described some popular reactions. While the examples thus cited certainly do not constitute a public opinion poll, the occurrences, according to eyewitnesses, were typical.

...I met a dye worker whom I knew, I asked him: "For whom are you going to vote tomorrow?" He answered: "I know only Ho Chi Minh, thus I'll vote for him..."

A barber also told me: "I will vote for Ho Chi Minh. As for the others I don't have to worry, for if I don't know them, the people at the election bureau must know them and will tell me for whom to vote."

A worker of the city water plant told me: "I didn't want to go out /and vote/ but my neighbor who is a member of the Tu-Ve (24) kept bothering me until I came out. Since I can't write, I'll ask someone at the election bureau to fill the ballot for me."

An inhabitant of Nam Dinh told me: "I already have voted on December 23rd (25) in Nam Dinh, but I wanted to see the elections in Hanoi and so, yesterday evening, I managed to get another voting card." ...and in another election bureau, a woman asked the three young girls sitting at a table: "Be so kind and write down for me the names of the ones I should vote for. I don't have much time for politics and don't know all the candidates." -- and this openly...(26)

The election results, though acclaimed a "brilliant success" by Viet-Minh sources, fail to show an overwhelming Viet-Minh majority. According to official statements of the Democratic Republic of Vietnam, the results were as follows, the figures apparently being incomplete: (27)

Marxists	10 seats
Socialists	27 "
Democrats	45 "
Dong Minh Hoi	22 "
VNQDD	26 "
Viet-Minh	82 "
Nationalist Independents	90 "

However, there are certain other points in which those elections proved to be unique. First of all, the National Assembly with its "elected" members convened six weeks before the election results were officially known and confirmed. Indeed, the Assembly met for the first time on March 2, 1946, while the official election results were published in the Official Journal on April 13! In view of the distances involved, the delegates from South and southern Central Vietnam who were present at the opening session of the National Assembly must have left their constituencies at the same time that the election ballots did. Furthermore, an even cursory inspection of the published election lists shows that the northern provinces which were under nationalist domination and where no elections had taken place (such as Vinh Yen, Viet Tri, Yen Bay, Lang Son, Dap Cau, and others) were nonetheless represented in the National Assembly by members or affiliates of the Viet-Minh. And lastly, while the approximately 17 million people of North and Central Vietnam were represented by 356 assembly members, the 5-1/2 million of South Vietnam were able to nominate only 18 delegates. (28)

It is hardly necessary to insist further upon the amount of caution with which one must consider the sometimes very enthusiastic reports that surround this particularly interesting facet of Vietnam's democratic political development.

A. <u>The National Assembly.</u>

The honeymoon period that followed the third agreement between the political factions hardly outlived the general elections. On January 13, the Provisional Government began to clear the hinterland of the Tongking delta by attacking Viet Tri, with attacks upon Phu To and Vinh Yen on the 20th, with little or no success in any case, the Chinese forces intervening on behalf of the DMH and VNQDD whenever the situation became too critical. In fact, the situation once more turned to the disadvantage of the Viet-Minh which also had to face a wave of unpopularity in its own ranks since the Provisional Government had to dismiss 75% of its employees in view of its desperate financial situation. The VNQDD, as the "Grand Old Party" of Vietnamese nationalism, celebrated the fifteenth anniversary of the abortive Yen Bay rebellion (10 February, 1930) in Hanoi with a parade of its armed forces and a greater amount of mass participation than ever before. For a time, Ho's regime seemed on the wane. However, here again luck was with the Provisional Government. Conversations had begun in Chungking between the French and the Chinese governments relative to the evacuation from northern Indochina of the 93rd and 53rd Armies and General Hsiao Wen, the Chinese political expert on Vietnamese politics, was recalled to Chungking on February 23rd. The remaining Chinese authorities limited their activities to the collection of "war booty" and intervened in Vietnamese affairs only when their own security seemed directly threatened.

From there on, the fate of the nationalist parties opposing the Viet-Minh was sealed. Violently anti-French, they could hope for little help from that quarter, while the Viet-Minh not only actively negotiated with the French but even succeeded in implicating the nationalist leaders in these negotiations, with the result that the aged Nguyen Hai Than resigned from his Vice-Presidency on the eve of the meeting of the National Assembly. (29) The Assembly officially convened at 8:00 a.m. on March 2, 1946, the day French detachments from China began their entry into upper Tongking. Ho Chi Minh immediately handed to the Assembly the resignation of his government. Ngo Tu Ha, the President of the Assembly and a Catholic, then proposed that Ho be entrusted with "...the mission of forming a Government of National Union. This proposal was adopted unanimously. Mr. Ho Chi Minh accepted, and, half an hour later, the Government was constituted." (30)

This new government, called the "Government of Union and Resistance," was composed as follows:

President: Ho Chi Minh*   Vice-President: Nguyen Hai Than (29)
Interior: Huynh Thuc Khang   National Defense: Phan Anh
Foreign Affairs: Nguyen Tuong Tam Economics: Chu Ba Phuong (31)
Justice: Vu Dinh Hoe*   Education: Dang Thai Mai
Public Health: Truong Dinh Tri   Finances: Le Van Hien*
Agriculture: Cu Huy Can*   Public Works: Tran Dang Khoa

*Known member of Indochinese Communist Party.

Furthermore, the National Assembly elected the other basic governmental bodies from among its midst:

a <u>Consultative High Council</u> with mere advisory powers under Nguyen Vinh Thuy - the former Emperor Bao Dai;

a National Resistance Committee, which in fact absorbed most of the
tasks of the Ministry of National Defense, so that the latter was
reduced to the role of a supply and procurement agency; Vo Nguyen Giap,
the Viet-Minh's military leader, was its chairman and Vu Hong Khanh,
an anti-Viet-Minh nationalist, became vice-chairman;

the Permanent Committee of the Assembly, which assumed legislative
functions between the regular legislative sessions along lines similar
to those of the Presidium of the Supreme Soviet of the USSR. Since
neither the National Assembly nor the Parliament designed to succeed
it met between 1946 and December, 1953, it was in fact the Permanent
Committee which carried the burden of legislation;

and finally a Select Committee for the Constitution, which was put in
charge of drawing up a Constitution of the Democratic Republic.

The Assembly dissolved that same afternoon at 1:00 p.m., and all members
of the Assembly who were not required for Cabinet or Committee assignments
were free to return to their constituencies.

A closer examination of the new Republican Government shows that Ho Chi
Minh had hardly relaxed his grip on the new administration. Having neutralized
the Ministries of Interior and Defense, he proceeded to transform the political
posts of the Youth and Propaganda Ministries into administrative services
which he could staff at will. Likewise, a decree of 22 March, 1946, allowed
Ho to appoint several under-secretaries of state of his own choosing: Interior,
Hoang Minh Giam; National Defense, Ta Quang Buu; Education, Do Duc Duc; and
others.

The beginning of the negotiations with the French both in Dalat and
Fontainebleau gave the Viet-Minh another chance to promote many of the
nationalists of other parties to conspicuous but ineffectual posts on the
conference delegations while certain key positions at home, which had been
relinquished under Chinese pressure, were returned to the Viet-Minh now that
the Chinese were departing. Thus, during Ho's absence in France during the
summer of 1946, it was the neutral Minister of the Interior Huynh Thuc Khang
who assumed the presidency while Vo Nguyen Giap took over the Ministry of
the Interior along with a newly-created Army Commissariat which was in effect
an embryonic general staff.

The arrival of the French in North Vietnam during the month of March
did not substantially change the government pattern of the Republican Government. The French at first limited their activities to the garrisoning of
troops in the various towns that had been assigned to them as a result of
the agreement of March 6, 1946, and the ensuing Franco-Vietnamese military
conventions. This gave the Viet-Minh a unique chance of liquidating whatever
was left of the nationalist opposition parties, since the latter were losing
their Chinese protectors and, thanks to their outspoken hatred of the French,
could not expect such support as the French gave to the Government after
March 6.

Thus, the Viet-Minh controlled Government forces occupied the whole
DMH-held area of North Vietnam during the month of June, 1946, and liquidated
the VNQDD strongholds in the Red River basin in July. Vu Hong Khanh, the
VNQDD leader, withdrew with a few hundred followers to the frontier post of

Lao Kay, which fell to the Viet-Minh in November, 1946. By mid-July, 1946, the Republican Government, unchallenged, controlled North Vietnam, most of Central Vietnam, and most of the countryside in South Vietnam. Politically the opposition had either fled to China or was in hiding. The only opposition newspaper which continued to appear in Hanoi was Viet-Nam, with an increasingly smaller circulation. Day after day, this VNQDD newspaper published lists of opposition leaders who had been arrested by the Government Security Service police, such as Hoang Ngoc Bach and Nguyen Bach Van, (32) Tran Quoc Lac and Hoang Tu Qui, (33) accused of being members of an underground gang called the "Bloody Hand," until on July 11, 1946, at 6:00 p.m., Vo Nguyen Giap, as acting Minister of Interior, began a vast mopping-up operation which lasted two days and culminated in the arrest of numerous opposition members and the temporary suspension of the newspaper Viet-Nam.

When this VNQDD opposition newspaper was authorized to reappear on July 18, with the same editorial staff as before, its front page editorial was devoted to a recognition of its past faults and a justification of the police operation carried out by the Republican Government. In the same issue of Viet-Nam, a VNQDD leader who had been in Ho's first government, Nguyen Van Xuan, called for a "renovated" VNQDD which would integrate itself into the Lien-Viet (United National Front) created by the Republican Government in May, 1946. Indeed, the opposition parties in the Democratic Republic of Vietnam had met the same fate as those in the People's Democracies.

B. The Constitution.

When the National Assembly of the Democratic Republic reconvened for its second session on October 28, 1946, the last it would hold until December, 1953, its former membership of 444 delegates had shrunk to a total of 291 present at the opening session. (34) According to neutral observers, (35) only 37 members of opposition parties were present on October 30, and upon a question by one of these, Cu Huy Can, the Viet-Minh Minister of Agriculture, answered that 33 opposition delegates had been arrested "...with the approval of the Permanent Committee, for common law crimes..." (36) The purges continued while the Assembly was in session, with the result that on November 8, 1946, date of the vote on the new Constitution, only two opposition members were left, while the number of pro-Government delegates had diminished to 240. (37)

Mass arrests had become commonplace enough to be openly admitted by even the quasi-official newspaper of the Republican Government. Thus, Cu'u Quoc ("National Salvation") of November 1, 1946, reported:

On October 29, our Security Services have, in the course of a raid, arrested more than 300 persons. After screening, the majority has remained in custody to be transferred to concentration camps.

It is in such an atmosphere of suspicion that the Constitution of the Democratic Republic of Vietnam was adopted by a vote of 240 to 2, and officially proclaimed on November 9, 1946 (see Appendix I for full text).

The Constitution gives a generally "Western democratic" impression to the reader in that it does not deal in economic theories and does not make use of stereotyped phrases, such as the "working people" or the "victory of the dictatorship of the proletariat," dear to the Constitutions of the Soviet Union or to some of the People's Democracies. As a matter of fact, neither does it resemble the new French Constitution of 1946, with its detailed social provisions (right to strike, collective bargaining, creation of an Economic Council). Like the Democratic Republic's Declaration of Independence, it appears designed to provide "reader appeal" in the Anglo-Saxon countries, and particularly the United States.

It provides for universal military training (Chapter II, Section A, article 5); equal rights for all citizens (II-B,6); protection and cultural autonomy for the ethnic minorities (II-B,8); equal rights for women (II-B,9); freedom of speech, press, assembly, religion, travel (II-B,10). Article 11 provides for habeas corpus in a simplified form and the subsequent articles of Chapter II, Section B, provide for freedom of education in private schools (with compulsory free primary education guaranteed by the state) and state assistance to the old and infirm.

Section C provides for universal suffrage by secret ballot for all citizens over 18, eligibility to public office for citizens over 21, and for constitutional amendment by popular plebiscite (Article 21).

Chapter III defines the role of the People's Parliament. It was to be a unicameral body, elected for three years at the rate of one member for every 50,000 inhabitants, with a special but undetermined arrangement for ethnic minorities and for the big cities. It was to elect its own President and two Vice-Presidents, together with a Permanent Committee of twelve regular and three alternate members, with the President and Vice-Presidents of the Parliament simultaneously assuming the posts of Chairman and Vice-Chairman of the Permanent Committee (Article 27). The Republican Government was far-sighted enough to realize that in operations during an uncertain future, a cumbersome legislature of more than 400 members would be hard to assemble, while the Permanent Committee -- though somewhat less than representative -- could be counted on to carry on the legislative work even under difficult circumstances. This explains the comparative lack of emphasis placed in the Constitution upon the Parliament itself while more than half of the constitutional articles devoted to the legislature are concerned with the attributes, functions, and powers of the Permanent Committee. Thus, the Committee was given many of the powers which the Presidium of the Supreme Soviet possesses. Part of Article 33 of the Constitution of the Republic reads: "The People's Parliament may dissolve itself... The Permanent Committee, in the name of the People's Parliament, shall proclaim such dissolution." Article 35 states: "... When the People's Parliament voluntarily dissolves, the Permanent Committee immediately proclaims re-elections. These re-elections must be carried out within two months after dissolution." Part of Article 47 of the Soviet Constitution of 1936 reads: "...the Presidium of the Supreme Soviet of the USSR dissolves the Supreme Soviet of the USSR and orders new elections." (38)

Article 49 of the USSR Constitution, which describes in detail the various powers of the Presidium, may be compared with Article 36 of the Vietnamese Constitution which authorizes the Permanent Committee to "vote on bills and decrees and other such projects" proposed by the "Government" -- a catch-all article under which the Committee has legislated since 1946. In fact, the Permanent Committee has certain powers which the Presidium of the Supreme Soviet (or any other such interim legislative body under other constitutions) does not possess: besides being able to convoke the Parliament, it may "control and criticise the Government," and, together with the "Government," "decide upon war or peace" (Articles 36 and 38). It is, therefore, obvious that whoever controls the Permanent Committee has a better than even chance constitutionally to control the country when the Parliament is not in session.

A Permanent Committee was elected during the November, 1946, session of the National Assembly and its membership reflected the Government's intention to find the Committee as receptive as possible to its wishes. Though resided over by a non-Communist, Bui Bang Doan, (39) it had six members of the ICP and two affiliates of the Viet-Minh among its fifteen members, while certain others, such as Cung Dinh Qui, (40) a member of the opposition, never claimed their position or participated in the activities of the Committee.

In their general aspects, the elections and appointments in the Government executive division closely resemble French parliamentary procedure, with the President and Vice-President to be elected from among the members of the People's Parliament (Article 44) by the members themselves. The same procedure is followed for the Premier, chosen by the President from among the Parliament members and approved by a majority of the latter. The Ministers in turn are chosen by the Premier, must be members of Parliament, and are nominated to the Parliament for approval. Only the Under-Secretaries of the various Ministries -- who would be mostly technicians -- may be chosen from outside the Parliament.

It may appear that the Government of the Democratic Republic of Vietnam as envisioned in its Constitution would be as much a subject to the whims of the Parliament as the French government, for example. This has not been the case in fact, however, since the Parliament has not met since the adoption of the Constitution and the interim functioning of its surrogate, the Permanent Committee, has insured perfect harmony between the executive and the "legislative" branches. Further, even if the Parliament had been functioning, Article 54 of the Constitution specifies that:

> A no-confidence motion may be deliberated by the Parliament only when proposed by the Prime Minister, the Permanent Committee, or a fourth part of the whole People's Parliament.

> Within a space of 24 hours after the People's Parliament has passed a motion of no-confidence in the Cabinet, the President of the Vietnam Republic is entitled to propose that the no-confidence motion be re-examined by the People's Parliament.

In other words, a motion of no-confidence would have to hurdle a number of constitutional barriers each of which is sufficient to make its chances of passage highly unlikely. Rare would be the occasion in which a Prime Minister would propose to the legislature to vote its lack of confidence in the cabinet he heads; the Parliamentary Permanent Committee was solidly in the hands of the governing administration; and it would not be easy to obtain a no-confidence motion supported by one-fourth of the whole Parliament, which on the basis of population would number over 400 members. Unless free elections returned a Parliament radically different from the 1946 National Assembly, it is clear that the executive branch would control the Government. (When the Constitution was adopted the National Assembly had never amounted to more than about 300 present members, and in the only vote which it was ever compelled to cast, that on the promulgation of the Constitution, it counted only two opposition votes!) In other words, as regards constitutional, parliamentary government, the stark political facts clash with the printed word of a text which, at first sight, seemed to bring all the guarantees of personal freedom, full representation with power, and political independence to a people subjugated for eighty years to foreign rule.

Constitutional questions dealing with local administration, the judiciary, and with the methods of constitutional amendment by popular plebiscite will be dealt with below in separate chapters on those subjects.

The foregoing exposition, it must be emphasized, presents only the theoretical aspect of the Constitution of the Democratic Republic. For on November 14, 1946, when the National Assembly closed its second meeting at a time of threatening political and military crisis, it decided to remain in its present form and not to transform itself into a parliament. (41) New elections for the regular People's Parliament were considered as "inopportune," so that the only constitutional legislative body which -- thus far -- has fulfilled its assigned duties is the Permanent Committee. Recent documents from the Viet-Minh zone, referring to the legislative sessions held by the Government of the Democratic Republic during the month of December, 1953, still refer to the "National Assembly" and not to the "People's Parliament." (42) Hence, it is safe to assume that the implementation of the Constitution of the Democratic Republic of Vietnam has remained at an indefinite or inchoate stage.

5. "Government-in-the Bush"

The activities of the Republican Government were soon to be overshadowed by the outbreak of general and open warfare with the French. The National Assembly approved on November 3, 1946, a new Government, with Ho Chi Minh occupying at once the posts of President, Premier, and Minister of Foreign Affairs, still flanked by his "Supreme Adviser," Nguyen Vinh Thuy, (43) with the Viet-Minh controlling the posts of the Presidency, Premier, Foreign Affairs, National Defense, Economics, Finance, Labor, Interior, Justice, Education, and Agriculture. The only cabinet posts which the Viet-Minh did not control at all were those of Public Works, Health and Social Security. Interpretations may vary as to whether the Viet-Minh was "really Communist" at that time. Nobody, however, can fairly contest the fact that it was on the road to one-party rule.

Likewise, the Presidium of the National Assembly (President and four Vice-Presidents) was ruled by Ton Duc Thang, an ICP stalwart of long standing. His position is the more interesting as -- while occupying the high posts of President of the Presidium and Vice-Chairman of the Permanent Committee -- his name does not appear on the list of elected members of the Assembly published in the Official Journal of the Democratic Republic on April 13, 1946. It is therefore most likely that he was directly appointed to either his membership in the Assembly, or to his high political posts. Likewise, the name of the new Minister of Labor, Nguyen Van Tao, is absent from the published lists of members of the Assembly.

In the meantime, with the failure of the Franco-Vietnamese negotiations at Fontainebleau, it became more and more apparent to the Republican Government that a solution to the political deadlock probably would have to be found in an armed clash while the French troops were still weak enough to make such an operation militarily feasible and politically desirable. On

November 20, fighting broke out at Haiphong, in the course of which the French
used their heavy artillery, with disastrous effects upon the local population.
On the other hand, the French point to a long list of incidents involving loss
of many lives on their side which had not been followed by retaliation. (44)
Nevertheless, the Republican Government began to fear a French surprise move
against its troops and against the Government itself. On November 26, 1946,
the various Ministries began to evacuate Hanoi, the capital. Defense prepa-
rations were in evidence in the city streets, and elements of the civilian
population began the evacuation of Hanoi and other cities. Each French
garrison, without being attacked, was progressively isolated from its neighboring posts by important road cuts, and within the city of Hanoi itself, the
various city boroughs were isolated by barricades and trenches.

When the attack broke out on December 19, 1946, it was a marvel of
coordinated planning. The general attack upon French garrisons in Hanoi was
preceded by sabotage of the electric plant, at 8:00 p.m., and was followed by
attacks against all French garrisons in North and Central Vietnam. (45) The
die was cast. Departing Hanoi, the Government of the Republic "took to the
bush." Both the French and the Democratic Republic of Vietnam grimly
settled down to a war that was to last longer than World War II.

FOOTNOTES

1. General Chang is reported to have served with Borodin in Canton in 1927 and is now back in the Chinese Communist fold. General Hsiao (sometimes spelled Siao) is also known under the Vietnamese name of Tieu Van.

2. Nguyen Ai Quoc, Proces de la Colonisation Francaise, Librairie du Travail, Paris, 1925. Nguyen Ai Quoc, alias Nguyen Than Than, alias Nguyen Sinh Chin, alias Ly Thuy, alias (since 1943) Ho Chi Minh, was born Nguyen Van Thanh on May 19, 1892, in Nghe An province (Central Vietnam), the son of an ex-mandarin. As ship's boy, he traveled extensively throughout the pre-1914 world (including the United States), and settled in France after World War I. He is known to speak "perfect" French, English, Russian, one or more Chinese languages, and several Indochinese languages and dialects. He became a member of the French Communist Party in 1920 and leader of the Comintern Coordination Committee for Southeast Asia in January, 1930.

3. Chinghsi is in Kwangsi Province, 60 miles northeast of Cao Bang. Also spelled Ching-hsi and Tsintsi.

4. Department of State, Office of Intelligence Research, Division of Research for Far East, OIR Report, No. 3708: Political Alignments of Vietnamese Nationalists, Washington, 1949, p. 63.

5. Celerier, Pierre (pseud.), Menaces sur le Vietnam, Ed. I.D.E.O., Saigon, 1950, p. 21.

6. Department of State, OIR Report No. 3708, p. 63.

7. Devillers, Philippe, Histoire du Viet-Nam, Ed. Seuil, Paris, 1952, p. 133. See also: Sainteny, Jean, Histoire d'une Paix Manquee, Amiot-Dumont, Paris, 1953, pp. 104 ff.

8. "The People's Liberation Committee of Vietnam" (Uy Ban Dan Toi Giai Phong Viet-Nam): President: Ho Chi Minh; Vice-President: Tran Huy Lieu; Members: Pham Van Dong, Cu Huy Can, Vo Nguyen Giap, Nguyen Dinh Thi, Chu Van Tan, Duong Duc Hien, Nguyen Van Xuan, Nguyen Luong Bang, Nguyen Huu Dang, Nguyen Chi Thanh, Pham Van Thach, Pham Ngoc Thach.

It is interesting to follow the careers of the various members of this initial "Committee" throughout the subsequent governmental combinations.

9. The "Provisional Government" of August 29, 1945:

President and Foreign Affairs	Ho Chi Minh*
Interior (Police)	Vo Nguyen Giap*
Propaganda	Tran Huy Lieu*
National Defense	Chu Van Tan*
Economy	Nguyen Manh Ha
Youth	Duong Duc Hien*
Social Security	Nguyen Van To
Justice	Vu Trong Khanh
Public Works	Dao Trong Kim
Finance	Pham Van Dong*
Hygiene	Pham Ngoc Thach
Labor	Le Van Hien*

9. (continued)

Education	Vu Dinh Hoe*
Without portfolio	Cu Huy Can*, Nguyen Van Xuan

*Members of the Indochinese Communist Party.

10. La Republique (Vietnamese weekly), Hanoi, 18 October, 1945.

11. Bulletin of the Vietnam-American Friendship Association, Hanoi, 1945, pp. 6-7.

12. L'Union Française (French daily), Saigon, 3 July, 1947.

13. See Sainteny, Jean, Histoire d'une Paix Manquée, Amiot, Paris, 1953.

14. New York Times, February 8, 1947; New York Herald Tribune, March 17, 1946.

15. Le Monde, 13-14 April, 1947; and Navile, Pierre, La Guerre au Viet-Nam, Editions de la Revue Internationale, Paris, 1949, pp. 201-206.

16. Ho Chi Minh had resided in China on a more or less permanent basis since 1925.

17. Considerations re. the Official Presentation of the Viet-Nam Worker's Party, November 1, 1951, Viet-Minh Document No. 13 in communication 1663-CD, June 5, 1953, Saigon, p. 5-6.

18. Official Journal of the D.R.V.N., No. I, Hanoi, 1945, p. 11.

19. Celerier, op. cit., p. 48.

20. Hammer, Ellen J., in L. K. Rosinger and Associates, The State of Asia, Knopf, New York, 1951, p. 238.

21. Vietnam Delegation in France, The Democratic Republic of Vietnam, Paris, 1948, p. 12.

22. There were no French troops in North Vietnam at that time. The first French troops landed in Haiphong on March 7, 1946, and entered Hanoi on March 18, 1946. However, French forces had landed in Saigon on September 23, 1945 and had occupied parts of Cochinchina (South Vietnam) in the following months in the face of strong continuing guerilla opposition.

23. After the Japanese coup, the complicated dike system of North Vietnam had been badly neglected which resulted in a nearly-total crop failure. The situation was further complicated by the absence of compensatory imports from South Vietnam and by the confiscation of rice by the Kuomintang armies. In the ensuing famine and epidemics between 800,000 and 1-1/2 million Vietnamese died in the north, according to common estimates at the time. Lucien Bodard, "Drame et Chances du Nationalism vietnamien," France Illustration, Paris, June 28, 1952, gives a figure of one million deaths.

24. The Tu-Ve were Viet-Minh Auto-Defense Units.

25. Nam Dinh, an industrial city and provincial seat 65 miles southeast of Hanoi, was one of the cities that had gone to the polls on December 23rd instead of on the official date.

26. Underscoring added.

27. Vietnam Delegation in France, The Democratic Republic of Vietnam, Paris, 1948, p. 13. The "Marxists" may represent "Marxist Study Groups" set up after the dissolution of the Indochinese Communist Party. The figures perhaps give the number attending the first National Assembly in March, 1946. The actual composition of the Assembly has never been made clear.

28. Celerier, op. cit., p. 52.

29. Despite his resignation and ensuing absence, Than was included in the government. He never participated in government affairs.

30. Vietnam Delegation in France, The Democratic Republic of Vietnam, Paris, 1948, p. 14.

31. Chu Ba Phuong, though an anti-Communist, was implicated in certain scandals which made him choose to remain on the Viet-Minh side after the December 19, 1946, clash.

32. Viet-Nam (Vietnamese daily), Hanoi, June 5, 1946.

33. Ibid., June 7, 1946.

34. French High Commission in Indochina, unpublished report, Saigon, 1951, p. 14.

35. Many Western correspondents were in Hanoi throughout the whole period.

36. Cu'u Quoc (Vietnamese daily), Hanoi edition, November 1, 1946.

37. Vietnam Delegation in France, The Democratic Republic of Vietnam, Paris 1948, p. 17.

38. Cf. Meisel, James H., and Kozera, Edward S., The Soviet System, G. Wahr Publishing Co., Ann Arbor, 1950, p. 249.

39. An aged man, Bui Bang Doan died soon after his appointment as President of the Permanent Committee, and was replaced by a Viet-Minh.

40. Cung Dinh Qui later on joined Bao Dai and became Agriculture Minister in the government of Bao Dai's Vietnam State under Nguyen Van Tam (1952-53).

41. Devillers, op. cit., p. 314.

42. Democratic Republic of Vietnam, Viet-Nam (weekly information bulletin) No. 2/54, issued at Rangoon, Burma, on January 14, 1954, p. 3.

43. The former Emperor Bao Dai resided in Hong Kong after March, 1946, and thus had no influence whatever upon the Republican Government, except that his name gave it an additional amount of international·and, for a time, internal prestige.

44. Celerier, op. cit., pp. 155-165.

45. Hostilities had practically never stopped in South Vietnam.

PART TWO: THE REPUBLIC AT WAR

1. General Observations.

In more than one way the outbreak of open hostilities greatly simplified
the economic and administrative problems which the Republican Government had
to face. Politically, the fact that the Republic was at war gave it excellent
grounds for simplifying the constitutional legislative and juridical apparatus
to the point where the functions of both were carried out by the executive.
The war situation also allowed the United National Front or Lien-Viet and
the Vietnam Workers' Party, Dang Lao Dong, or DLD, through their control of
local unofficial "Resistance Committees" to assume governmental and administrative tasks of ever-increasing importance. The Lien-Viet is a Government
front which was developed to include all patriotic social and political
organizations in the Republican area. The Viet-Minh was merged with the
Lien-Viet in 1951 and thus technically disappeared; however, the term Viet-
Minh has continued in general use both in Vietnam and elsewhere. The Workers'
Party was created in February, 1951, to succeed the old Indochinese Communist
Party which was supposedly dissolved in 1945.

Likewise, the stalemated situation of the war gave the Republican Government a good opportunity to shake down its cadres, to evolve a certain administrative policy, in short, to "settle down" in the everyday business of governing
the land in the fullest sense of the word. Thus, most of the now-existing
governmental organs in the territory controlled by the Democratic Republic
have undergone very little change in the past few years; a fact which permits
a more detailed study of their organizational structure and probable long-range
effects upon the future political evolution of Vietnam (1).

2. Local Administration in the Democratic Republic.

When the Provisional Government of Ho Chi Minh first gained control of
North and Central Vietnam during the summer of 1945, it found there the
traditional administration as preserved with little modification by the French
colonial administration, with its councils of notables (sometimes elected but
mostly appointed and hereditary) and elders, presided over at the provincial
level by a French administrator. Stable (or stagnant) as it was, this
machinery had continued to work even after all the French personnel had been
interned by the Japanese, since the small Vietnamese village is generally
autonomous by tradition and self-sufficient by economic necessity. (2) The
arrival of the young revolutionary elements of the Viet-Minh in the villages
had the effect of the proverbial stone in the village pond. In the words of
Pierre Gourou, one of the most respected French experts on Indochinese affairs,
"armed adolescents have replaced the peaceful councils of notables. This is
not necessarily an improvement." It certainly was a drastic change and, in
less than eighteen months, did more to alter the political-administrative
aspect of the Vietnamese countryside than did the Vietnamese emperors since
938 A.D. or the French since 1862.

While the first attempts at local administration on the part of the
Viet-Minh were haphazard, the very fact that village autonomy was so deeply
rooted made an ideal breeding ground for the type of local administration
found in the early post-revolutionary years in the Soviet Union. Indeed,
"the decentralizing policy practiced by the Revolutionary Government presented
great analogies with that applied by the communist Government of Soviet
Russia." (3)

As stated in the Constitution of 1946 Vietnam was divided into three
main administrative units (Bo), with each Bo divided into provinces, prefectures,
districts, villages, quarters (i.e., boroughs), and urban areas. The lower
territorial units (up to province) elect People's Councils "by direct
suffrage" (Art. 58), which in turn elect their own executive committees; while
the higher echelon units (Bo and "Inter-Zones," or Lien-Khu, which, though not
mentioned in the Constitution, have become major territorial units) only elect
an Executive Committee by the indirect vote of the People's Councils of its
subordinated territorial units.

It is in this particular section of the Republican Constitution that the
parallelism with the Soviet system is quite apparent:

...the general assembly of the Soviet elects from its membership an
executive committee.... In localities the administrative power belongs
to the Soviets, in whose jurisdiction must be all the institutions of
administrative, economic, financial and educational characters....
All previous orders of local governments...must be replaced by respective
(regional, provincial and county) Soviets. (4)

Similarly the functions of the committees closely follow those described
by Lenin in The Rights and Duties of Local Soviets with but minor differences.
An extremely detailed description of the various local administrative bodies
with their relationships and functions was published in the form of a decree
on November 22, 1945, i.e., a full year before the promulgation of the
Constitution. (5) These bodies all had certain common characteristics: first,
there was a uniform two-year tenure of office; second, eligibility requirements
were liberally interpreted; and third, differences over election results were
settled administratively by the next higher echelon. At every echelon, there
was a deliberating body directly elected by the population, the Hoi-dong Nhan-
dan or Popular Assembly; and an executive arm elected by the Popular Assembly
from among its own members, along French or Soviet parliamentary methods of
procedure, namely the Uy Ban Hanh Chinh or Administrative Committee. (6)

The Village Popular Assembly (Hoi-dong Nhan-dan Xa) generally contains
10 to 25 members and 5 to 7 alternates, depending upon the size of the community.
Voting requirements are similar to those of the general election but include
in addition a residence requirement of three months prior to the election date.
Military and administrative personnel assigned to a given village are considered
residents regardless of length of actual residence. Eligibility requirements
for candidates include a six-months residence in the village and no exception
is made for military and administrative personnel wishing to participate in
the election.

The Provincial Popular Assembly (Hoi-dong Nhan-dan Tinh) has 20 to 35
members and 5 alternates, with each district (huyen) represented proportionally
to its population. All voters registered on the village rolls within the
province are automatically eligible to vote and, surprisingly enough, there
are no residence requirements (Art. 35). The law does not specifically
authorize military and administrative personnel to participate in such elections,
but this seems to have been a mere oversight on the part of the legislators.
In actual practice, such personnel fully participate in local and national
politics, as under the Soviet system. (7)

Municipal Popular Assemblies (Hoi-dong Nhan-dan Thanh-pho or Hoi-dong Nhan Thi-xa): the Regional Administrative Committees (8) were given the power to create or to dissolve municipalities (9) and eight cities were given autonomous municipal status throughout Vietnam: Hanoi (the capital), Haiphong, Nam-Dinh, Vinh, Ben-thuy, Hué, Da-nang (better known under the French name of Tourane), and Saigon-Cholon. Voting requirements were the same as in the village assemblies and eligibility requirements were as liberal as those of the provinces. Military personnel were specifically authorized to vote and to be elected. (10)

The Administrative Committees (Uy Ban Hanh Chinh), as stated above, constitute the executive branch of local government at every level, but at the same time, must "carry out orders issued by higher authorities," e.g., the central government or the next higher territorial echelon. The Administrative Committee is "responsible to higher authorities" before it is responsible "to its own People's Council." (11)

There were generally five echelons of Administrative Committees: the three named above and the district and regional committees whose duties were at first strictly administrative and which were elected not by the population at large but by the administrative committee of the subordinate territorial echelons. (12)

The Administrative Committees had the following characteristics: (1) Each had one chairman, one vice-chairman and one secretary. (2) All were elected by indirect suffrage, with separate elections for the three above-named posts, with the exception of the Regional Committee, where all elections took place at the same time in one single vote. (3) Tenure of office is generally two years, with the exception of the Regional Committee's, where the tenure is three years. City borough (thanh pho) committees are elected for one year. (4) Conditions of ineligibility or incompatibility include husband and wife, a parent and two children, three brothers or sisters on the same committee. Likewise, while military and administrative personnel were eligible, they could not retain their official functions while serving on the Committee. (13) There are, however, strong indications that the latter regulation is not strictly observed. (14) (5) The Administrative Committees are generally quite small. At village level they include five members including its president, vice-president, treasurer and secretary and a commissar in charge of security matters, as well as two alternates. At district level, there are only three regular members and two alternates. The Provincial and Municipal Committees are similarly organized. The Regional Committee, like the local committees, has five regular and two alternate members.

While it cannot be denied that the various local administrative bodies were originally endowed with wide powers within their territorial limits, those powers were progressively curtailed as the Republican Government consolidated its position in the country. A circular from the Ministry of Interior (whose powers resemble more those of the Soviet Ministry of Interior than those of the U.S. Department of Interior) specifically states that all orders and regulations issued must be in full accord with similar decisions of every higher echelon, a provision which practically nullifies whatever legislative power there was in the hands of the local assemblies except on very narrow local issues. (15)

Likewise, even on local issues any decision taken by a local unit of government has to be passed on to the next higher echelon for approval, and is inoperative in the meantime. If after a delay of five days, the District Committee (in the case of a village) has expressed no objection, the decision becomes operative. However, in the case of a decision affecting communal property, the tacit agreement of the higher echelon is not sufficient and specific approval has to be secured. Some questions considered strictly local matters from the Western point of view (local taxes, budget, public works, etc.) even require approval of the next higher echelon, the Provincial Administrative Committee. (16) In turn, provincial administrative tasks require the ratification of the regional authorities -- with a fifteen-day delay before implementation -- and the region cannot approve the majority of the legislative acts of its provinces without prior referral to the full Council of Ministers. (17)

The cumbersome nature of such an administrative structure is obvious. Indeed, it successfully amalgamates the worst aspects of rule by committee with those of "democratic centralism" while the paucity of communications and trained personnel soon creats administrative bottlenecks at the higher echelons, thus seriously disrupting the national governmental process.

To sum up, the committees at various echelons have the duty to control the activities of the subordinate committees and assemblies; to approve certain decisions made by subordinate levels of administration; and (in the case of the regional committees) to decide appeals of the communal administration against decisions of the provincial authorities, and to promulgate the legislation necessary for regional application of nationwide decisions of the central government. Also, both the regional and the provincial committees have the right in an emergency to call on the help of the armed forces stationed in their territories -- subject, of course, to later endorsement of the measure by the central government.

The departure of the Government from Hanoi in late December, 1946, did not immediately bring about a change in the administrative structure of the territory controlled by the Republican Government. A few months later, however, the need for both a strong integration of the whole population into a system of total war and for better ideological control brought about the suspension sine die of the Popular Assemblies and the "merger" of the Administrative Committees at every echelon with the local unofficial "Resistance Committees."

In other words, every administrative committee -- and many at that time were still not entirely in the hands of the Viet-Minh -- was manned simply by a cadre of appointed political officials. The new committees thus created were named Uy Ban Khang Chien/Hanh Chinh (UBKC/HC) or "Committees for Resistance and Administration," followed by the unit of its administrative level (UBKC/HC xa or Village Committee for Resistance and Administration; etc.).

As the war spread over greater areas and many sectors fell into French hands during the early stages of the campaign, the Republican Government decided to create administrative units that were integrated with the military commands, particularly in sectors contiguous to French-held areas. This brought about the creation, on an informal basis at first, of "zones" (khu) and groups of villages, districts or provinces, i.e., territories adjoining territorial units lumped together under a single administrative authority generally articulated with the local military command zones. These units are known as "Inter-Zones," "Inter-Provinces," "Inter-Villages," etc. (Lien-khu, Lien-tinh, Lien-xa, etc.) The region (ky) seems to have been abandoned as an administrative unit in favor of the zone (khu) and inter-zone (lien-khu). (18)

One cannot say, however, that government by legislation has entirely disappeared from the territory of the Republic. According to Viet-Minh reports in January, 1954, the National Assembly of the D.R.V.N., which had not met since 1946, convened in North Vietnam during the first week of December 1953. Out of 444 members, 177 attended and ratified the land reform decree of May 20, 1953, which thus becomes the law of the land.

The Republican Government still seems to rely upon popular elections for the nomination of the administrative members of the various UBKC/HC. A decree of February, 1948, (19) shows that the committees of Vietnam were classified into three categories according to their political reliability:

Category A. Villages entirely under the control of the Government. Universal suffrage should be applied to them (if it does not hamper the good execution of military operations).

Category B. Villages not entirely under the control of the Government, or (though within the controlled zone) could not participate in universal suffrage without gravely prejudicing military operations (résistance). Only persons of both sexes belonging to People's Troops (Dan Quan) or National Salvation (Cu'u Quoc) units may participate.

Category C. Villages situated in enemy territory....

Three years after the outbreak of the hostilities, the Republican Government apparently accepted the idea that the war was going to be protracted, and promulgated a special set of regulations designed to reinstate the Popular Assemblies in a somewhat streamlined form. A series of decrees on the "Organization of Power during the Period of Resistance" (20) contains, substantially, the following innovations:

Article XII. Should the Communal Popular Assembly make a decision contrary to higher orders, this order is not only annulled...but the UBKC/HC of the district will issue a warning. Should the Communal Assembly refuse to comply, the Provincial UBKC/HC may pronounce its dissolution.

Article XIII. After dissolution of the Assembly, the provincial UBKC/HC...shall designate a provisional committee....

The two texts do not show whether the designated committee would eventually be replaced by a new elected committee. Other articles take cognizance of the increasingly difficult situation in transmitting legislation for higher approval and the various transmittal periods are therefore increased from five to eight days (Article XXIV) (21), while another article now specifically provides for higher approval of the nominations of UBKC/HC chairmen at all levels (Article XXXIV).

The same decree provides for the reorganization of the UBKC/HC on a new basis; at local level, three members of the committee are selected from among council members after prior approval of the next higher UBKC/HC; two other members -- including a Military Affairs Commissar -- are designated by the provincial UBKC/HC. Thus, by nominating two of the three members of the village council and by specifically choosing the local UBKC/HC chairman, the higher authorities are always assured of at least a 3-2 majority should the question of refusal to comply with higher orders ever arise. No such case is on record.

The administrative load falling on the average village in the Republican Government zone exceeds anything a community of similar size would have to bear anywhere outside the Iron Curtain and seriously burdens the available personnel. In one typical example, the Tien Hai district in North Vietnam, the UBKC/HC chairman assumes "full responsibility" for everything; the vice-chairman is in charge in the absence of the chairman and is also the town "sheriff"; the secretary is in charge of all the paperwork and keeps the minutes of the committee sessions; together with the chairman and vice-chairman (the secretary acting as recorder) they constitute the judicial committee, the basic unit of the judicial system. (22)

One member of the committee is in charge of the finances; another of "economic problems" (direction of the village cooperative and checking of goods smuggled in from the French Union zone); a third, of People's Troops, guerillas and the watch service; a fourth, of education, public works and road maintenance. The District Committee found that the fourth man was not fully occupied and in addition entrusted him with running the compulsory labor service of the village.

There can be no doubt that the average Vietnamese villager, already harassed by his unusual struggle with the elements to earn his livelihood and by the ever present threat of enemy air raids or ground attacks, has lost much of his erstwhile eagerness to participate in the festive occasions of political meetings, elections and discussions.

The Republican Government had to find out for itself that elections and meetings can be too much of a good thing and that, past a certain point, agricultural work and war production would suffer. The switching of such meetings to night hours, while it afforded additional protection against air raids, also deprived the farmers of sorely-needed hours of sleep. Certain districts soon reported that a good part of the population considered an election as a sort of "compulsory labor." On the other hand, a report from Hadong province in North Vietnam (a province that is theoretically almost entirely controlled by French Union and Vietnam Nationalist forces) shows that during the 1951 elections for the provincial UBKC/HC, 33,336 voters out of a registered 51,517 went to the polls. (23)

Still, there can be no doubt that the Republican Government under the control of the Viet-Minh has succeeded in establishing at least the sub-structure of what could have become a decentralized democratic government. It is too early to say whether the experiment failed because of the lack of adequate cadres or because it was never meant to succeed. There is probably some truth in both assertions. As early as May, 1946, the lack of trained personnel compelled the Minister of Interior to detail to every district and provincial committee a Hiep-ly (Assistant-general) (24) to assist it in the regular performance of its duties, and today Can-bo (cadres) expert in financial, administrative or military matters are detailed to the various administrative echelons to help insure a minimum of efficiency. (25) At the same time, it is certain that such "help" also implies control over the local administration by the Central Government.

3. The Judiciary of the Republic.

The Constitution itself gives but a limited amount of information on the judiciary of the Republic. It mentions a Supreme Court of Appeals, intermediary Appeal Courts and Provincial and Prefectoral Courts. All judgeships are appointive, and trial by jury exists on an advisory basis for misdemeanors and on a voting basis for felony cases. Lastly, the Constitution expressly states that no other authority is allowed to interfere with the functions of the judiciary.

Thus far, no fully new code of justice seems to have developed and the law applied is sometimes the old French Code. The Code of Military Justice of the Democratic Republic is an almost verbatim copy of the French original. Generally, however, trials, particularly those of enemies of the state, are held on a completely informal basis, with the public supplying most of the arguments as well as a good part of the final judgment.

In view of the situation, it was the Military Courts-Martial (Toa-an Quan-Phap) which were created first, by a decree of September 13, 1945, and developed by subsequent decrees which expanded their jurisdiction but hardly modified their initial qualities of expediency and harshness. (26) Crimes liable for prosecution before the courts-martial were those of "attempts against the independence of the Democratic Republic of Vietnam." The presiding judge is always a member of the armed services; the first judge a delegate of the Communist, later Workers' Party, and only the second judge is a professional jurist. The prosecutor may be an officer, a member of the Security Police or a professional magistrate (27). The defendant has the right to counsel; he may defend himself or may ask the presiding judge to appoint counsel on his behalf (28).

The courts-martial may pronounce five types of sentences: (a) simple acquittal; (b) confiscation of parts or all of defendant's property; (c) prison from 1 to 10 years; (d) hard labor from 5 to 10 years; and (e) the death sentence. Confiscation of property may be pronounced concurrently with any of the other sentences, which greatly contributes to the solution of the landowner problem. All but the death sentences are final, with no further possibilities of appeal, and the death sentence is carried out immediately after rejection of the appeal. The presiding judge must inform the defendant of his right to appeal and the record must show that the defendant had been informed of this privilege, lest the trial be considered void.

A. Military Tribunals.

Oddly enough, the Military Tribunals (Toa-an Quan-Su) are presided over by a civil servant, assisted by two members of the armed services. Like the code itself, court procedure is similar to that of French military tribunals. As in the case of the courts-martial, appeal authority appears to exist only in the case of capital crimes.

B. The Civil Court System.

As Chart I shows, the civil court system is not separated in fact from the other branches of government. Nor is it divorced from the authority of the Workers' Party, since the UBKC/HC which is instrumental in the appointment of the lay judges, is subordinated both to the executive branch of the Govern-

THE VIET-MINH JUDICIARY

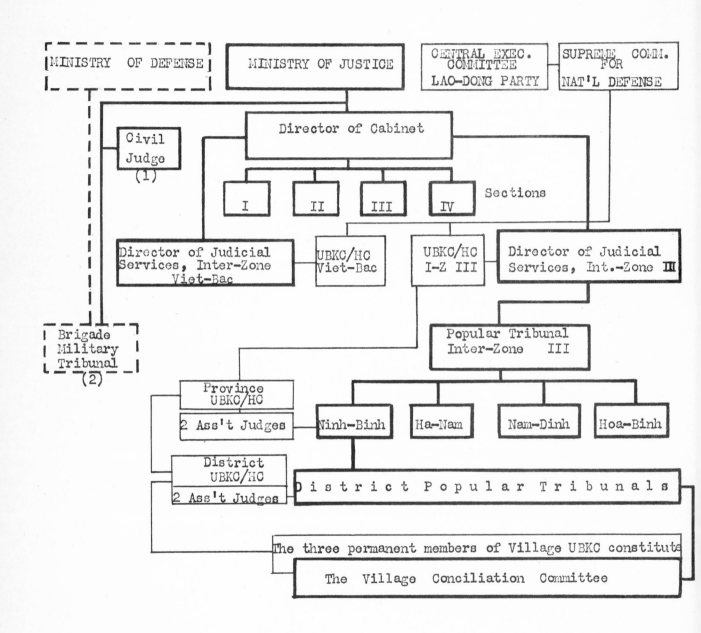

LEGEND

– – – *Defense Ministry Channels*

—— *Judicial Channels*

—— *Party-Administrative Channels*

<u>Note</u> : On this chart, judicial services
are fully developed for Inter-Zone III
only.

(1) There is a civilian judge at
    every level of military juris-
    diction.

(2) For the sake of simplicity,
    the military court system was
    not further developed on this
    chart.

ment and to the Central Executive Committee of the Party; both are represented in the Supreme Committee for National Defense.

Civil courts exist at every level of territorial administration, and in each case above the village the respective UBKC/HC appoints the two lay judges of the three-man court, the presiding judge being a professional jurist. There exists only one court of appeals per khu (zone) and its decisions are final. It is, however, at the village level that the impact of the Government and the Party upon the judiciary is most felt: the three-man Village UBKC/HC is the primary court itself. It is hard to imagine how under such circumstances one could sue the village with any chances of success.

C. Supreme Court.

The supreme judicial authority of the Democratic Republic has but little in common with what is known as a "Supreme Court" in other parts of the world. While it may receive only a very few civil cases—since most of the subordinate courts already have final jurisdiction in such matters—it has a wide range of investigative powers. To that effect, it is armed with a special "Inquiry Commission" which is authorized to "...control the work of all civil servants, People's Committees and all organs of Government..." (29)

The Supreme Court is in fact not an autonomous body. It has two judges, the President of the Republic and the Minister of the Interior, with the Minister of Justice acting as the recorder. The post of prosecutor is held by one of the members of the Inquiry Commission. There is, of course, no further appeal authority and all judgments, including the death sentence, are carried out within forty-eight hours. The Supreme Court of the Democratic Republic appears to be in charge of primary jurisdiction in the case of high treason of cabinet members or high-ranking army officers.

D. Trials by Administrative Decision.

While the tribunals enumerated above may not deviate too much from certain other simplified court systems existing under conditions of stress in other countries the role of administrative decision in arrests and detentions, which the Democratic Republic has raised to a veritable system, strikes a familiar ring to anyone acquainted with similar methods of "progressive popular" justice in other authoritarian states.

> In cases where the tribunal receives a complaint, or is itself acquainted with the existence of a state of arrest which it has not requested, the Public Prosecutor shall enquire with the Administrative Committee. Should the Administrative Committee inform the Court or reply that the arrest has been made for a political motive, the Tribunal will cease to pursue the matter..." (30)

A further technique is provided for such cases that reach the Court but do not receive the desired sentence. In such a case, when

> ...the words or acts of the suspect could be prejudicial to the struggle for independence, to the democratic regime, to public tranquillity or national union, the police will transmit the file to the Chairman of the Administrative Committee for consideration regarding a final solution of the case...." (31)

Thus, there is hardly a loophole left for criminals to slip through, except perhaps the always present possibility of a mistrial. That matter was soon taken care of by a sharp reminder of Hoang Quoc Viet, the powerful leader of the Vietnam General Confederation of Labor, the government-backed labor union, to the judges at all echelons, bringing to their attention that their main task consisted in "putting out of commission the enemies of the people, and not, by applying to the letter some obsolete text, to let them escape from just punishment for their crimes..."

E. The New Code of Justice.

A National Justice Congress (Hoi nghi Tu Phap Toan Quoc) was held in 1950 in the Inter-Zone III (North Vietnam), which brought about the adoption of a simplified version of the French Civil Code and some small revisions in the organization of the existing courts. The simplifications seem above all to be the result of the lack of trained personnel to staff all courts with professional judges. A system of "People's Assessors" was introduced at every level of jurisdiction, with greatly extended powers. They hold a preponderant vote in court, have the right to inspect the files of the cases at hand, and may make their decisions upon perusal of such documents before or during the trial, regardless of whether or not the documents were introduced in court.

Another interesting feature in the new judicial system is that the Director of Judicial Services at lien-khu or zone level, the Giam-doc Tu Phap, acts as prosecutor at the Popular Tribunal of the Inter-Zone (Toa-an Nhan-dan Lien-khu). Under the new code, military tribunals are now entirely subordinated to the Ministry of National Defense. The presiding judge is now the commanding officer of the local regiment, with one judge designated by the Ministry of Justice and the third drawn from the provincial administration.

In any case, the role of the career magistrate seems to have been reduced to that of a technical adviser. Likewise, reversals of judgment for reasons of mistrial were purely and simply abolished, a fact which no doubt greatly enhances the claim of infallibility of the Popular Courts. Likewise, a serious blow was dealt to a great number of possible libel suits by introducing a very generous element of permissible error in all cases of denunciation to the police:

> The law orders every citizen to report all violations to which he is
> a witness. Therefore, the citizen who has denounced...by error and
> without intention to do harm, cannot be held guilty... One should not
> take into account the old custom which inflicted on the denunciator
> the same punishment which would have been received by the denounced
> person. (32)

There can be no doubt that the new code emphasizes a radical departure from generally accepted standards of jurisprudence. This development is even more visible in the treatment accorded defense counsels who seem to be the last hapless remnants of formalistic jurisprudence in the Democratic Republic. The new system allows for a defendant to call upon "...a simple citizen, not /necessarily/ a barrister, to take his defense..." (33), while a more recent circular emphasizes that "the tribunals should do their utmost /to see/ that favor be given to defense counsels chosen from among the simple citizenry..."

Private defense counsels who have accepted to plead a case for a fee have been prosecuted themselves for "abuse of confidence," while, for the time being, court-appointed counsels receive an indemnity.

F. The Courts as an Executive Weapon.

Recently, special popular tribunals have been created in order to enforce the new land reform. Under the new law repressing "Sabotage of the Agrarian Reform" (34), any sentence up to and including the death sentence may be pronounced and judgments are executed on the spot.

The change of line is apparent throughout the whole judicial system now and, strangely enough, the Democratic Republic sees to it that such changes receive widest attention. In a very recent issue of the government's official newspaper, such an example of progressive people's justice was clearly demonstrated:

> ...Before, the judicial committee of the community of Phuc Xuan worked in the authoritarian manner of civil servants. Now, the working methods have entirely changed. After having pronounced sentence, the tribunal solicits criticisms from the population. A farmer has made the following remark: 'I may state that since the tribunal is democratic, it shows itself indulgent towards the people and energetic towards the reactionary land owners.' (35)

And as if to dispel any doubts as to the type of energy that is now usually displayed by such tribunals, the official radio network of the Democratic Republic broadcast on September 15, 1953, excerpts from an article on the subject:

> ...the comrades got together and decided to judge the most cruel of the land owners. Knowing what conduct to adopt, what arguments to present, what witnesses to call, the comrades enthusiastically took their measures to help with the judgment that was to take place the following day...
>
> Having learned their lesson from preceding trials, no barriers were erected to separate the land owner from the farmers. There was but a human wall to encircle the enemy... The trial began animatedly. More than thirty persons rose from the ranks to denounce the crimes of the cruel and reactionary landowner Phu Thanh Y: dishonest ruses...gouging...ill treatment and murders... Besides these crimes, the comrades and farmers accused Y of having shown himself hostile to the Government and to have slandered the Party and the Government...
>
> Y's face was pale, his body shook; Y sat down on the ground and remained silent with terror for several minutes... One could see that he was more than mastered. (36)

This is by no means an isolated case, and the newspapers and radio broadcasts of the Democratic Republic -- for reasons unfathomable to the Western mind -- continue to relate the minute details of such trials for the edification of friend and foe alike. It is quite obvious that under conditions such as those described above, the legal rights of the individual who lives in the zone controlled by the Government of the Democratic Republic of Vietnam cannot be considered as guaranteed, even by the greatest stretch of the imagination.

FOOTNOTES

1. I wish to acknowledge here my debt of gratitude to Dr. Vu Quoc Thong, Professor at the Administrative School of North Vietnam and at the Law Faculty of the University of Hanoi, for his help and guidance in evaluating and collecting the material used in the following chapter; and to draw attention to his remarkable study on the Vietnamese administration: Vu Quoc Thong, La Décentralisation Administrative au Viet-Nam. Presses Universitaires du Viet-Nam, Hanoi, 1952, 400 pp. (mimeo.).

2. An old Vietnamese proverb states: "The power of the Emperor stops at the bamboo hedge." (Each village is generally circled by a bamboo hedge.) See also Paul Mus, "The Role of the Village in Vietnamese Politics," Pacific Affairs, 22 (1949): 265-272, and his excellent book, Viet-Nam, Sociologie d'une Guerre, Sevil, Paris, 1952.

3. Vu Quoc Thong, op. cit., p. 295.

4. See Provisional Workers' and Peasants' Government, Gazette, No. 21, St. Petersburg, January 6, 1918.

5. Viet-Nam Dan-quoc Cong Bao (Official Journal of the Democratic Republic of Vietnam), Vol. I, Decree No. 63, November 22, 1945, pp. 131-197.

6. For the reader unfamiliar with Vietnamese administrative units, the following are the most recurrent: xa (village), huyen (district), tinh (province), thi xa ("big village," e.g. city), khu (zone), and ky (region).

7. See also Appendix I.

8. There are three regions (ky) in Vietnam: North, Central and South.

9. Democratic Republic of Vietnam, Official Journal, Vol. 1, 1945, Article 1 of Decree No. 77, December 21, 1945.

10. Ibid., Article 6.

11. D.R.V.N., Constitution, Chapter V. Articles 59 and 60.

12. Vu Quoc Thong, op. cit., p. 296.

13. D.R.V.N., op. cit., Articles 64 and 65 of Decree No. 63, November 23, 1945.

14. Even at the highest echelon, there are elected members of government filling at the same time administrative posts: Ton Duc Thang, President of the Permanent Committee, is at the same time Special General Inspector of Political and Administrative Affairs; and one of his colleagues on the Committee, T. Q. Phiet, is at the same time Chairman of the Administrative Committee at Quang-Nam.

15. D.R.V.N., Official Journal, Article 66 of Decree No. 63, op. cit. See also Appendix II.

16. Ibid., Article 70.

17. Ibid., Article 85.

18. See Map 3, p. 87.

19. Document captured by French Union Forces in Gia-dinh province (South Vietnam) on May 10, 1948. Parentheses in original text.

20. D.R.V.N. Decree No. 254/SL of November 11, 1948, and Regulation No. 82/SD of March 13, 1949.

21. This excessive paperwork constantly traveling to and fro throughout Vietnam is one of the major sources of French Union intelligence. Lately, local Republican authorities have complained against this degree of "bureaucratism," but apparently with little success.

22. See Appendix II and sections on the judiciary below.

23. The Viet-Minh report fails to state, however, that there are about 600,000 inhabitants in that province.

24. D.R.V.N., Official Journal, Vol. II, May 11, 1946, p. 309. The decree also specified that appointees had to have been members of the higher or secondary cadres of the French colonial administration.

25. The Can-bo are discussed in Part Five below.

26. D.R.V.N., Official Journal, Decrees 77b and 77c of 28 December, 1945, 7, 21 of 15 January and 14 February, 1946; Regulations No. 60b, 60c, 79, 82, 125 and 146 of February, April and May, 1946.

27. Ibid., Decree No. 21, 14 February 1946.

28. Ibid., Regulation No. 82, 25 February 1946.

29. Ibid., Decree of November 25, 1945.

30. Interministerial Circular No. 208 NV/PC, May 27, 1946.

31. Ibid.

32. D.R.V.N., Penal Code, 1950, Article 373.

33. Ibid., Decrees 69/SL of 18 June, 1949 and 144/SL of 22 December, 1949.

34. D.R.V.N., Official Journal, Decree 149/SL or 2 April, 1953.

35. Cu'u Quoc, daily newspaper, September 18, 1953.

36. Xuan Truong, article in Nhan-Dan, daily newspaper, No. 131, of August 26, 1953, transmitted over "Voice of Vietnam" North, on 15 September, 1953.

PART THREE: THE PARTY IN POWER

1. The End of the Viet-Minh.

As noted above, the Dong Duong Cong San Dang (Indochinese Communist Party) voluntarily dissolved itself on November 11, 1945. The task of Communist proselytizing was transferred to an "Association for Marxist Studies" created to that end while the political and military work of the party was transferred to the Viet-Minh with its affiliated National Salvation (Cu'u Quoc) organizations embracing old and young, the farmers and the soldiers, the townspeople and the women, etc., and whose leadership was almost entirely recruited from among the old ICP leaders.

However, it was soon found that the Viet-Minh was not sufficiently supple in carrying out the decisions of the leaders, not for reasons of ideological divergences but rather because of the large size of its membership. It was then decided to re-create a distinct political party around which could be built a well-disciplined following. This was to be the aim of the absorption of the Viet-Minh into the Lien-Viet, the United National Front. (1) The Central Executive Committee of the Lien-Viet was presided over by Ton Duc Thang, who, according to a Communist source, was one of the mutinous sailors that participated in the famous Black Sea rebellion that made André Marty famous. For this, he served nineteen years in Indochina's ill-famed Poulo Condore island penitentiary (2). Among the other twenty-seven members of the committee there were at the outset twelve Communists and six affiliates, so that there can be little doubt as to the general leanings of the United National Front. This process of absorption of the Viet-Minh (which, one must remember, still contained the remains of other Vietnamese splinter parties, such as the "renovated" VNQDD and DMH and Socialist Parties) was very slow and gradual and was only completed during the "Congress of Unification of the Lien-Viet and Viet-Minh Fronts" held early in March, 1951 in North Vietnam. (3) Once this process was completed and the various subsidiary organizations of the Viet-Minh solidly integrated, the leaders of the Democratic Republic proceeded to re-create a hard inner core of politically trained and reliable citizens. The Viet-Nam Dang Lao Dong (Vietnam Workers' Party, or DLD) was born.

The birth of the Workers' Party was announced to the country at large one month after it had taken place, during a meeting of the old leaders of the ICP, February 11 to 19, 1951:

> In the course of those eight days of work, the Congress has received reports on administrative, military, economic and financial questions; on the activities of the Viet-Minh Front; on the patriotic emulation campaign, and on the life of the working people and the ideological struggle.
>
> The Congress has adopted the resolutions, its action program, its statutes and a resolution concerning the work of the Party and has elected the Central Executive Committee of the Workers' Party of Vietnam. (4)

Retrospectively, it must be emphasized that the Government of the Democratic Republic actually took a full five years (1945-1951) to transform the regime openly into what appears now a "model satellite"; and still today, the Government has maintained a certain number of non-party members, or members of other parties, in cabinet positions. This, however, is not exceptional, since non-party members also hold such positions in certain other People's Democracies.

Quite the contrary, it is a correct application of the Instructions voted by the IVth Congress of the Comintern as applying to underdeveloped areas:

> ...instead of creating a single national-revolutionary party based upon individual adherents, one must attempt to co-ordinate and to unite the activities of the various national-revolutionary organizations with the help of common action committees, so as to create an effective bloc of all revolutionary elements. (5)

For all practical purposes then, the Viet-Minh, like the ICP, had disappeared. However, the name of "Viet-Minh," hated, feared or admired, was to become part and parcel of the myths of the D.R.V.N.

2. The Vietnam Workers' Party in Operation.

It is hard to fathom at first whether the re-appearance of an openly Marxist-Soviet party in Vietnam in 1951 should be considered as a proof of the assertion that by then the Communist element of the Viet-Minh was solidly in control of the country and could afford to shed its nationalist camouflage; or whether its re-appearance at Ho's will at that date shows proof of Ho's relative independence from the Soviet bloc. Such an allegation, which would actually confirm the "relative independence" theory, is drawn from a Soviet source of 1947:

> ...the decision to dissolve the /Communist Party in Vietnam/ was /due to the/ bitterness on the part of many Vietnamese Communists against the French Communist Party and the international Communist movement because of lack of support of their independence aspirations. (6)

Yet according to a French source, the ICP had in fact never ceased to exist (7) but had merely performed a "strategic retreat" so as to assure the fledgling Democratic Republic as wide a sympathetic audience as possible (which, in fact, it had until the hardening of the "Cold War" front lines during the Korean war). Moreover, Viet-Minh sources indicate the Party's strength as 20,000 in 1946, 50,000 in 1947, and 168,000 (!) for 1948; broken down in 102,000 members for the Bac-Bo (North Vietnam), 43,000 for Trung-Bo (Central Vietnam) and 23,000 for Nam-Bo (South Vietnam). Figures for 1950 show a total membership of approximately 500,000 to 700,000. This latter figure seems excessively high and probably includes numerous Lien-Viet organizations. (8)

It is obvious that the new DLD was not conceived to be such a mass movement. It was definitely meant to become the major instrument of governmental and political power, with several improvements over the former ICP. The new line was soon apparent in a confidential circular issued by the Executive Committee for the Nam-Bo on March 28, 1951:

> ...we may tell the Party adherents that the new party is basically the Communist Party under a new form; but to those that are outside of the Party, we will say that is is a newly-created party merely continuing the revolutionary work of the preceding parties. (9)

Among the external trappings of the old ICP, the DLD maintained the old party banner, but here again, it seems that the Democratic Republican Government desires a certain toning-down of the party emblems. In an official circular of the Army of the Democratic Republic, it is definitely stated that while

...the flag of the Party is still the red flag with sickle and hammer
...that flag will only be flown on the occasion of meetings of the
Party Committees and not publicly. (10)

In view of the foregoing, there can be little doubt as to the similar
nature of the DLD and the former ICP except that the old ICP was too doctrinaire,
too abstract to become a good tool for mass control. This fact was readily
acknowledged by the DLD leadership and the Constitution, or Party Charter of
the Viet-Nam Dang Lao Dong reflects the desire on the part of the DLD leadership to create a "less advanced" party. This makes the comparison of the
DLD Party Statutes with those of the Communist Party of the Soviet Union
(Bolshevik) (CPSU(B)) and of the Chinese Communist Party (CCP) quite
interesting reading.

A. The Statutes of the Workers' Party.

In its preamble, the DLD Statute reads:

> ...The basis of the DLD and its guiding line in all fields of its
> activities is the doctrine of Marx, Engels, Lenin and Mao Tse-tung,
> adapted to the realities of the Vietnamese revolution. (11)

One can readily see that the DLD left itself a sort of "mental reservation"
clause by conditioning the acceptance of the Communist doctrine to its adaptation
to local conditions. The non-inclusion of Stalin among the great teachers of
Communism and, conversely, the inclusion of Mao Tse-tung, seems to be either
an oversight or a gesture of good-will to People's China, whose CCP dutifully
excludes J. V. Stalin from its list of Communist augurs while it includes
Mao (12). On the other hand, the DLD's oversight is partially repaired by
assigning its members to

> e) - deploy all their efforts to elevate their level of thinking by
> studying the doctrine of Marx, Engels, Lenin and Stalin, and the
> thoughts of Mao Tse-tung. (13)

The same "scaling-down" from the CPSU(B) to the CCP and, at a somewhat lower
level again, the DLD, can be found throughout various articles and statutes.
And again, this strict party-political hierarchy can be observed in the
relations between the Vietnam Workers' Party and the even "younger" revolutionary
parties of Cambodia and Laos. Whereas the CPSU(B)

> ...exercises the leadership of the working class,...of the entire
> Soviet people, in the struggle for the consolidation of the dictator-
> ship of the working class,...for the victory of Communism (14),

the CCP's revolution

> in the present stage must take the form of a new bourgeois-democratic
> revolution-- that is, an anti-imperialist, anti-feudal, new democratic
> revolution of the masses under the leadership of the proletariat (15);

and the DLD's struggle is, at a lower level, only

> popular and democratic, whose mission is to eliminate the invading
> imperialists, to suppress the remains of feudal and semi-feudal rule;
> and to realize the principle 'to each his own piece of land'... (16);

while Cambodia's Revolutionary Party merely

> unites the whole people in the Issarak Front, to collaborate closely
> with the Vietnamese and Lao peoples...and to carry on a firm struggle
> so as to annihilate the French colonialists, the American intervention-
> ists and their puppet lackeys... (17).

It would be pedantic to go into the other details of the DLD Statutes.
But even a cursory examination will show that they hardly differ from those of
the CPSU(B) -- except organizationally, since the CPSU statutes apply to a
federal state, while Vietnam is a centralized republic -- and from those of the
CCP. They are closer to the latter, however, in view of the similarity of
problems involved: existence of a "national bourgeoisie," residual feudal
elements, and an agrarian reform problem of first magnitude. With but minor
exceptions the situation of the Democratic Republic of Vietnam may be compared
to the "War Communism" period of the U.S.S.R. in the early 'twenties.

As a general rule, the Party Statutes of the Vietnam Workers' Party
cannot be considered as too accurate a picture of the actual work done by the
party in the country. One may safely affirm -- as will be shown below -- that
the Statutes overstate the political importance of the DLD while they seriously
understate its administrative importance as a vital arm of the D.R.V.N. Government in the furtherance of its policies. This is more apparent in the
"Manifesto and Platform of the Vietnam Workers' Party" (18), in which appears
an interesting set of priorities:

> Special care shall be taken to raise the material standard of living
> and cultural level of the army...

> The workers who are production fighters...shall have their living
> conditions improved...

> The peasants who are production fighters...shall benefit from the
> reduction of land rent and interest rates, and from appropriate
> agrarian reforms.

> The intellectual workers shall be encouraged...

> Small-scale trades and small workshop owners shall be assisted...

while the national bourgeoisie shall receive "guidance"; the "patriotic landlords"
shall be authorized to collect rents; national minorities shall be treated on
a footing of equality; while further "effective help" was assured to women,
religion, overseas Vietnamese citizens, foreign residents and particularly
Chinese; close union was also promised the Khmer and Lao peoples, the Soviet
Union, China, the People's Democracies, and the peoples of France and her
colonies -- the whole in that order of enumeration.

B. The Organization of the Workers' Party.

There are in fact only two major changes in the organizational structure
of the DLD as compared with that of the ICP: it has a separate Political Bureau
(Politburo) and a Party Inspectorate; two organs which the former ICP did not
possess. It has a Central Executive Committee (Ban Chap Hanh Trung Uong) of
nineteen members and ten alternates. The members in March, 1953, were:

VO NGUYEN GIAP, Minister of
Defense and Commander-in-Chief

TRUONG CHINH, Secretary General
of the Lao Dong Party

PHAM VAN DONG, Vice-President,
Head, D.R.V. Delegation to the
Geneva Conference

TON DUC THANG, President of
Lien-Viet Front

HOANG QUOC VIET, President of
the V.N. Labor Union

NGUYEN CHI THANH, President of
the V.N. Youth Federation

President of DLD.............................. Ho Chi Minh
Secretary General of DLD...................... Truong Chinh
Chief, Political Bureau of the Ministry
   of National Defense........................ Nguyen Chi Tanh
Political Commissar and acting Commander-
   in-Chief, South Vietnam.................... Le Duan
Minister of National Defense and
   Commander-in-Chief......................... Vo Nguyen Giap
Vice-President of Government................... Pham Van Dong
Director of Current Affairs................... Le Duc Tho
Director General, National Bank............... Nguyen Luong Bang
President, Vietnam Labor Federation........... Hoang Quoc Viet
President UBKC/HC Bac-Viet..................... Chu Van Tan
Acting President of National Assembly
   Permanent Committee........................ Ton Duc Thang

Member, Lien Viet National Committee......... Le Van Luong
Director General of Supply, General Staff
   of the Vietnam People's Army............... Tran Dang Ninh
Ambassador to People's China and Member of
   the Lien-Viet National Committee.......... Hoang Van Hoan
President of UBKC/HC Lien-Khu III............. Le Thanh Nghiem
-                                 .... Tran Van Hoan
President UBKC/HC Lien-Khu V and Inspector
   of the Central Government for Lien-Khu V.. Nguyen Duy Trinh
Director of Current Affairs of the
   UBKC/HC Nam-Bo............................. Pham Hung
Deputy-President UBKC/HC Nam-Bo and
   Southern Zone............................. Ung Van Khiem

Of these members of the Central Executive Committee of the Party, the following held also extra-Committee positions: Truong Chinh, President of the "Marxist Study Group" and member, National Committee of the Lien-Viet Front; Nguyen Chi Tanh, President of the Youth Federation and member, Lien-Viet National Committee; Le Duan, Special Secretary, Workers' Party Southern Command; Vo Nguyen Giap and Pham Van Dong, members, Lien-Viet National Committee; Le Duc Tho, Central Government Inspector for the Southern Zone Command; Nguyen Luong Bang, in the fall of 1953, Ambassador to the U.S.S.R.; Hoang Quoc Viet, Vice-President of the Lien-Viet; Chu Van Tan, General, Vietnam People's Army and member, Lien-Viet National Committee; Ton Duc Thang, Inspector-General, Government Inspectorate and President, Lien-Viet National Committee: Pham Hung, Chairman, Workers' Party Central Executive Committee for South Vietnam and Chairman, Workers' Party Central Office, Southern Zone.

From the above it is easy to see that the Vietnam Workers' Party's Central Executive Committee not only controls the affairs of the Party but also is able to control the administration of the country (through its members who are also Presidents and Vice-Presidents of Inter-Zone UBKC/HC's), its military forces (through the Minister of Defense and Commander-in-Chief) and its foreign relations (the D.R.V.N.'s only known ambassadors are members of the Central Committee). It also controls the "non-partisan" organizations and activities grouped in the Lien-Viet Front by its numerous members who double also as members of the National Committee of the Lien-Viet.

As Chart II shows, the Vietnam Workers' Party is strongly centralized in structure. The various deliberative assemblies have had no occasion to exercise their functions. The National Assembly of the DLD was called in November, 1953, for the first time since the inception of the Party to approve the land-reform law which had been promulgated in May, 1953, under the form of a decree (19); and to "put into effect the slogan 'Land to the Tillers' ..." (20). However, the given schedules of the various Party assemblies is as shown below.

Level	Interval between Ordinary sessions	Interval between Executive Committee sessions	Party Membership Tenure*	
			Member Executive Committee	Secretary General
Central	Three years	Six months	U n d e t e r m i n e d	
Zone and Region	18 months	Six months	Four years	Six years
Province, Municipal Area	18 months	Six months	Three years	Four years
Huyen	12 months	One month	Two years	Three years
Village, Borough or Plant	Three months	One month	Undetermined (One year?)	Two years
Cell Group	One month	15 days		One year

* Tenure in the ICP is cumulative with DLD tenure.

As a comparison with the corresponding sections (V through VIII) of the Charter of the Communist Party of the Soviet Union shows, major differences occur only at intermediate levels, where the difficulties of traveling in war-torn Vietnam are most felt and had to be taken into account by the creators of the DLD statutes.

One important facet of the organization of the DLD is the grouping into cells of individuals of the same profession. Not only must a DLD member of such a cell (Dang Doan) obey the normal party rules, but he must also serve the best interests of his professional "inter-group" by forwarding all relevant information in his own field to the next-higher echelon. This system permits a very efficient cross-checking of practically every step of the execution of a directive, according to the specialty of the Dang Doan, and conversely, allows for the practically immediate implementation by political discipline of an order of administrative, political or military nature. Information forwarded by the Dang Doan is handled by the competent technical committees on the DLD staffs at municipal, provincial or regional level.

With the merger of the political and administrative authorities within the Uy Ban Khang Chien/Hanh Chinh (see page 24), the Workers' Party organization received a quasi-official mandate to consolidate its control upon the various territorial administrative levels. In the words of the "Handbook of the Indochinese Communist Party," 1948 Edition:

> In fact, the Administrative Committees hold their power under the control of the Chi-Bo representing the executive power, whose Dang Doan may represent one of the organs of execution.

In its own curious way, the Democratic Republic seems to practise the Marxist principle of the "withering-away of the state" by replacing or capping state organs by a party machinery that frequently is far more complex and comprehensive than the administrative or executive organ which it parallels.

C. Party Organization within the Armed Forces.

A similar situation of tight political control of the command machinery exists in the armed forces of the D.R.V.N. (see Part V). Vietnam Workers' Party cells (Chi-Bo) exist at all levels, and the General Political Commissar (Tong Chinh Uy), Nguyen Chi Tanh, is the right-hand man of the Commander-in-Chief.

The Central Military Executive Committee is directly co-ordinated with the Central Executive Committee (Tong Chinh Bo, or "Tong-Bo") of the DLD, and in turn directly controls the Political Commissariat of the General Staff of the Ministry of National Defense (Dang Bo Quoc Phong Tong Tu Lenh). Technical services centralizing the actions of the Dang Doan, the Cadre Council of the Specialized Branches (Infantry, Artillery, Engineers, etc.), and the Council of Combatants (in charge of discipline) are also directly subordinated to the command cell group. Subordinate cell-branches (Lien-Chi Chi-Bo) function under the three Commissariats of the central echelon:

a. Commissariat for the General Political Directorate (Dang Bo Chinh Tri) controlling an Administrative Office; the Bureau of Chinese Affairs (i.e., within Vietnam); and Counter-Propaganda.

b. Commissariat for the Army General Staff (Dang Bo Tram Muu) controlling the cells of the Administrative Office; the General Headquarters; the General Staff of People's Troops (i.e. guerillas); Liaison and Communications; Engineers; Service Schools; the Inspector General's Office; Intelligence (Quan-Bao); and Military Justice.

c. Commissariat for the Director General of Military Supply (Dang Bo Cung Cap) controls the cells and inter-cells of Quartermaster Supply; Medical Troops; Matériel; Arsenals and Armament Plants; and Ammunition and Explosives Depots.

"Civilian" party control merely steps in in the case of the Technical Committees of the Dang Doan whose competence overlaps in both the civilian and military fields. At regional and local levels, the Party organization is channeled from the Dang Bo Tram Muu (General Staff Cell, see (b) above) directly to the Political Commissar at Inter-zone (Lien-khu) or Brigade (Su-Doan) or Division (Dai Doan) level. At regional level, the organization of the Central Military Committee of DLD repeats itself at a lower, inter-cell, level. Instead of the three above-mentioned commisariats, there are three Lien-Chi Chi-Bo:

a. Command Inter-Cell (Lien-Chi/Chi-Bo Tu-Lenh) controlling cells in Brigade Staff; Communications; Intelligence; Military Justice; Service Schools; and HQ Troops.

b. Armament and Services Inter-Cell Branch (LC/CB Quan Gioi) with cells in the Regional Arsenals; Depots; Armament Plants; Medical Services; Quarter-master units; Supply Services, etc.

c. Regimental Inter-Cells Branches (LC/CB Trung-Doan) which are the most important cells at that level since they control the whole political apparatus of their subordinate units (battalions, companies, platoons and squads). The whole machinery repeats itself once more at regimental level, with lien-chi at battalion and company level; chi-bo at platoon level; and, finally, cells of party members (tieu-to) at squad level.

It is obvious from the above that the DLD possesses a workable machinery to control the Vietnam People's Army as an integrated part of its own body politic. The corps of Political Commissars, established as a part of the regular Vietnam People's Army (21) at the same time as the official creation of the army itself, effectively completes the total stranglehold which the Workers' Party has upon the armed forces of the Democratic Republic.

3. Ideological and Psychological Warfare.

Like all Marxist parties, the Vietnam Workers' Party greatly stresses the importance of political indoctrination and guidance at every level of the political, cultural and economic life of the country. It also has succeeded remarkably well in making abundant use of psychological warfare upon its adversaries and also upon neutral nations by means of publications, propaganda hand-outs and radio broadcasts. Within its own ranks, recurrent sessions of self-criticism, indoctrination, and ideological discussion contribute to the creation of a coherent block of "correct thinking" members, while similar tactics used upon the population at large assure the D.R.V.N. government of a large following that is at least willing, if not enthusiastic.

A. Internal Propaganda.

The propaganda addressed by the regime to the population under its control concentrates on the various topics that are foremost in the minds of the government and Party policy makers: (1) the war effort; (2) increased production both in the war industries and on the land; (3) land reform and the elimination of the landowners; (4) furtherance of the Marxist ideology as expressed by the Lao Dong and the Lien Viet.

In order to co-ordinate the propaganda efforts throughout the country, conferences are held from time to time to expound the general line of the government's propaganda of the moment. The latest in date seems to have been held in the south (Nam-Bo) in June 1952. Among the directives then adopted were the following:

To propagandize is to mobilize and to educate the population so as to make it hate the enemy; so that it shows ardor in national reconstruction and is fully confident of the final victory.../the people7 have in their hearts love for the fatherland, hatred for the enemy, and the will to win. The people are ready to go about their

tasks. The cadres are here, furthermore, to act in accordance with
the feelings that animate the people. (22)

The statement goes on to say that such results may be best obtained by a
careful selection of the news presented to the population:

> The information /services/ must collect everything that concerns the
> living conditions of the population; and the atrocious crimes committed
> by the French and their puppets. The latter information will be grouped
> and collected by the Special Service prior to being disseminated anew
> among the people. ... The secret /propaganda/ centers must concentrate
> upon simple and very precise news which shall bring the masses to
> comply spontaneously with the directives of the propaganda. (23)

Such simple slogans are generally expounded during one of the many festivities
of the regime. Thus, on the Thousandth Day of Resistance (June 19, 1948) Ho
Chi Minh launched the first such nationwide slogan: "To Create Bases and
Break Records"; the 1950-51 slogan was "Increase Production in spite of
Difficult Conditions"; the 1951-52 slogan advocated, "Facilitate the Edification
of Economic Bases of the Regime of Popular Democracy"; the 1952-53 slogan exhorted the people "To compete in Ardor to Accomplish Exploits"; while the
1953-54 slogan merely exhorted them "To continue to perfect the Mission of
strongly preparing for the General Counter-Offensive." The most recent slogan
seems to have been the "Land-to-the-Tillers" which became popular during the
most recent sessions of the National Assembly and the National Conference of
the Lao Dong, in December, 1953. The ubiquity of such slogans, once they are
adopted, is hard to imagine. They will appear in streamers across the streets,
painted along the walls of houses; and at the beginning and at the end of
practically every official communication, no matter what its contents.

The "hatred" theme seems to be given a marked preference in the pro domo
propaganda. An editorial of the semi-official Cu'u Quoc is quite revealing:

> ...To struggle victoriously, we must study until we are impregnated
> with the policy to be followed, we must concentrate our thoughts and
> deeply meditate upon our misfortune, upon the way we have been oppressed
> and pilfered...
> When we shall have discovered the bottom of our misery, we shall
> feel an even deeper hatred... By telling each other our misfortunes,
> we will feel them better; and the more we shall feel them the stronger
> will be our hatred, the more efficacious will be our struggle... (24)

Such a deliberate whipping-into-frenzy is no isolated instance; examples
of the same line can be found at every level of Viet-Minh propaganda. It
seems now to be a potent weapon used in the anti-landowner campaign. A
particularly instructive case was reported over the D.R.V.N. radio, relating
the liquidation of a rich landowner at Quang Binh (Hoa-Binh Province) who
hitherto had been left undisturbed by the local UBKC/HC:

> ...To end this situation, the Party and Government sent to Quang
> Minh a delegation of cadres specialized in agrarian questions...
> On September 4 /1953/ meeting from 9 o'clock to 5 o'clock on the
> following morning, nearly 5,000 peasants denounced /the landowner's/
> crimes and forced him to submit to popular will. (25)

Anyone even vaguely familiar with the habits of farmers in general is rather inclined to doubt that five thousand farmers would spend on their own volition eight solid hours of sorely-needed sleep in a propaganda session. The method used is the same which has been used in China, and results in implicating the local population to the point that it fears the reprisals (often-occurring) of the Franco-Nationalist troops for acts committed in its name by the outside "specialized cadres." In its majority, the peasant population then supports the regime because it is persuaded that it has no other alternative (26).

One other main theme is that of work emulation, and production successes are pointed up as examples in newspapers and over the Republican radio network. The examples quoted, however, are impressive in their puerility and incredibility. It will strike Western minds as admirable only if true that Bac Giang Province had overpaid its rice taxation quota by 62 per cent; and that the French-occupied Lien-Khu III went over its quota by 12 per cent; and the Viet-Minh's Thanh-Hoa stronghold topped its quota by 99.3 per cent (27). The fact that 10,000 farmers in Son-Tay Province collected six tons of insects in ten days (28) will prove more amusing, since the per capita daily quota would amount to about 2-1/2 oz. of insects, or two grasshoppers per farmer per day...

The third main subject of internal propaganda, French atrocities, also defeats its own argument by sometimes overstating its own case. While the picture of guerilla warfare is a sorry one per se, a Viet-Minh newspaper found it necessary to report that at My Loc sixty French soldiers had raped seven hundred women in one afternoon (sic); and that the French -- by means of scientific feeding and an electric treatment -- transform the slightly-built Vietnamese into huge Senegalese infantrymen... (29)

B. Viet-Minh Propaganda in the Vietnam Nationalist Areas

The means which the Republican Government has at its disposal to carry out psychological warfare in the zones held by the French Union Forces and the Vietnam National Army are considerable. Its most important weapons are its radio stations. There are five specifically Republican transmitters:

a. Voice of Vietnam, broadcasting in Vietnamese, Chinese, Thai, English and French. The station's northern transmitter also broadcasts in Cantonese, in addition to the other languages.

b. Voice of the Nam-Bo, probably installed aboard a junk on the Mekong River, broadcasts in Vietnamese, Mandarin Chinese, French and Khmer (Cambodian).

c. Voice of Free Saigon-Cholon, also a mobile station, in Vietnamese and Cantonese.

d. Voice of the Resistance, purports to transmit from Hanoi, but actually transmits from adjoining Viet-Minh territory, in Vietnamese.

e. Voice of Free Cambodia, operated by the Viet-Minh's Command Office, South, broadcasting in Vietnamese and Khmer.

In addition, Radio Peking and Radio Moscow beam very powerful broadcasts in Vietnamese to the area (30). The Viet-Minh also operates a network of six Morse code services connecting the Republican Government with its agencies in

People's China and Burma, and with the Information Offices (in charge of propaganda) in North Vietnam, South Central Vietnam (Lien-khu V), Saigon-Cholon and Nam-Bo. The stations under the control of the D.R.V.N. achieve a high record of regularity, and have thus far escaped destruction. French "jamming" is only partially successful. The propaganda themes beamed at the areas under control of the Franco-Nationalist forces concentrate on the military successes of the Republican forces and on the corruption alleged to exist within the ranks of the National Government:

> ...What is a government which has put a price upon everything? It is scandalous that a young recruit in the Vietnam National Army can escape front-line duty for 20,000 piastres, or may escape the draft by paying 40 to 80,000 piastres to a high-ranking officer of the General Staff in order to obtain a passport to the United States or to France. (31)

Strangely enough, in the same broadcast, the Viet-Minh accused the National Vietnam Government of "religious persecution" and cited as proof for such assertions the fact that troops of the politico-religious sects in South Vietnam had deserted the ranks of the National Armed Forces (32).

Another important facet of the Republican propaganda effort against its adversary is euphemistically named "Armed Propaganda." It actually consists in outright terror and intimidation of officials and prominent citizens of the Nationalist zone. Special units (Dich-Van) operate in certain fringe areas, such as Cambodia, or on special missions where ideological sabotage of a given target area is particularly important. A standard Dich-Van unit will have a Commissar for Current Affairs, a Commissar for Propaganda-Education, one other in charge of Patriotic Competitions; two secretaries and about twenty armed men. Their action is at times highly efficacious, and seriously affects Nationalist control at village levels. To quote but one typical example, in the last five months of 1952, in the Than-Ha huyen of the Dong-Trieu hill area in North Vietnam, the Viet-Minh killed or kidnaped 52 notables, including 17 village chiefs and two borough chiefs. It is obvious that after a repetition of that "treatment" in a certain area, the Vietnam National Government is unable to find adequate cadres for its local administration, thus leaving the countryside entirely in the hands of the Viet-Minh.

There are, however, cases in which propaganda and even "armed propaganda" seem to fail, such as in the Viet-Minh's attempts to sabotage the local and provincial legislative elections in the areas under control of the Vietnam National Government. Despite intimidations and threats, the electoral turn-outs can be termed satisfactory. The Viet-Minh propaganda groups themselves ascribed their failure to the following causes:

> Completely vague understanding of our can-bo concerning the importance of the last elections (which are preparatory to nationwide elections;

> 2. Lack of firmness and delays in the spreading of propaganda among the masses to denounce the clever policy of the enemy;

> 3. Lack of initiative in counter-propaganda during the election period, so as to pillorize the unworthy candidates;

> 4. Lack of reaction after the elections to point up the frauds, to unmask the unworthy electees.

The following remedies were recommended in the case of further elections:

> 1. Necessity to follow in a continuous way enemy activities in the matter of elections...so as to report back to the unit, which will establish a systematic sabotage plan.

> 2. Necessity to intensify without let-up the popular propaganda to unmask the candidates and to annihilate their popularity...

> 3. To report back to the unit the social status of the candidates, their tendencies, ambitions and their attitude towards our enemies. (33)

The above examples should suffice to show that the propaganda services of the Democratic Republic and of the Lao Dong party are anything but a haphazard affair. Their impact upon the population under control of the Vietnam National Government cannot be denied. The Viet-Minh propaganda services also make abundant use of conventional propaganda media, such as leaflets, magazines and newspapers, whose impact upon the great masses of newly-literates is hard to estimate. Apparently, the "fight-illiteracy" program of the Democratic Government seems to have fulfilled its promises (34), so that the written propaganda exercises an influence that is actually greater than generally expected. Therein lies an even greater likelihood for the success of such propaganda, for

> men who have just been taught to read, to write and to count are only likely to be better slaves, and it is harder to defend people against semi-culture than against ignorance. For there is 'reading' and reading. Reading is nothing if one cannot distinguish between the truth and the lies printed on a piece of paper, and if one cannot recognize the secret combinations which they may form at times. (35)

C. Propaganda in Favor of People's China and the Soviet Union.

An important part of the more recent propaganda is devoted to extolling the benefits which the Republic derives from being associated with the Soviet Union, People's China, and the other "People's Democracies." In order to further such propaganda, particularly in fringe areas between zones and in zones with strong Chinese minorities in which resentment against the Chinese is strong, a "Vietnam-China-U.S.S.R. Friendship Month" (36) was launched on January 21, 1954, anniversary of the death of Lenin. The following text describes a relatively small festivity in a Viet-Minh-held area of South Vietnam: (37)

The Vietnam-China-U.S.S.R. Friendship Month in the Nam-Bo

(Report on the inauguration of the Friendship Month on January 21, 1954.)

All the villages have a festive air. Everybody has made it a point to come to the rally.

At the end of the day, on the roads, groups converge towards the village carrying signs on their shoulders or in their hands. Bicycles circulate in every direction; barges and sampans are to be seen everywhere on the river. More than 2,000 persons participate in the meeting: compatriots, members of associations, the military, etc.

All have their eyes fixed on the photographs showing the reconstruction of the U.S.S.R. and of China--the Berlin Festival (38) and the combats along the border... The photographs of the "Old Father" (39) are respectfully admired. These photographs show him crossing the forest and the mountain regions of Cao-Bang and Langson in disguise; he is on his way to inspect the front lines.

Other members of the associations have stopped in front of a painting showing the life and struggle of the great Lenin and of Stalin. This painting has been recently sent from the U.S.S.R. After the opening which followed the usual ceremonial, the conference proceeds with the election of the honorary presidents. President Ho, Mao and Malenkov are unanimously elected...

The comrade Tran Ba Khan of the section of Arts and Letters of Nam-Bo speaks first. He explains the important significance of the Friendship Month which has opened on January 21, the day of the anniversary of the death of the great Lenin. The whole audience rises and observes a minute of silence in the memory of the benefactor of humanity while the speaker retraces the valorous deeds of that great man. After this, Mr. Ca Van Binh rises to the rostrum in order to read the telegrams sent by the friendly countries at the occasion of the Friendship Month. This is greeted by general enthusiasm.

Then Mr. Ung Van Khien reads the inauguration speech. He shows the glory of our people since its recognition by the U.S.S.R., by China and by the other People's Democracies. "Our nation," says he, "is the equal of all other nations." He also speaks of the solid friendship of the U.S.S.R. and of China, of the immense aid which these countries never cease to give us... /He says/ that we must take example upon the U.S.S.R. and China from three viewpoints:

1. The ardent spirit of patriotism, the international spirit of the proletariat;

2. The spirit of struggle of long duration and of autarky.

3. The position of the different /social/ classes and the experience of the agrarian reform.

"And finally one capital point is the edification of the bases for an association Vietnam-U.S.S.R. and Vietnam-China, in the Nam-Bo."...

Mr. Ca Van Binh then rises again to the rostrum to present under every angle the economic, cultural, political and military reconstruction of the two leading countries: the U.S.S.R. and China...

Speaking of the inauguration of the Berlin Festival he made the following description: "Dozens of national flags floated in the wind; among them our beloved national flag of Vietnam. The red flag with the yellow star floated in the sky of the German capital. Thousands of cries rose, millions of exclamations were shouted by a whole generation of youth that had come from hundreds of countries throughout the whole world: "'Peace to Vietnam! Long live President Ho Chi Minh!'" and the speaker continued, "What an honor for us and for our country, sons and nephews, descendants of the goddess and of the dragon." (40)

The comrade Ca Van Binh descends from the rostrum. One could have heard a needle drop; such was the silence of the audience, absorbed by what they just had heard.

Mr. Lam Lap, delegate of the Chinese nationals in Nam-Bo, gives his own impressions of this festivity. He speaks in Chinese language of the smashing victory of the strenuous and lengthy struggle of the Chinese people to find again its sovereignty... Then he speaks of the intimate connections between Vietnam and China... He recalls that all Chinese nationals of Nam-Bo are in close solid union with the Vietnamese and asks the latter not to consider them any more as foreigners...

"The Chinese citizens must effectively participate in the military, political and administrative activities; must pay the same agricultural taxes, industrial and commercial fees, fight side by side with the People's Troops so as to defend our houses and to struggle against the common enemy; the French colonists and the American interventionists. In such a way we shall become worthy to be citizens of New China, of the generation of Mao Tse-tung."...

Before closing the main part of this meeting, several messages were sent to the Soviet and Chinese people, President Ho Chi Minh and to the Organization Committee of the Friendship Month. After the salute to the flag, the evening show of the Arts and Letters program begins. It has been made possible, thanks to the efforts of the national cadres, the Chinese citizens and all the other members who present artistic and literary work of the Soviet Union and of People's China.

From the foregoing it is obvious that such a well-orchestrated propaganda must have an undeniable influence upon the illiterate or newly-literate masses of Vietnam, and it is likely that its long-range effects upon the population both in the Republican and in the Nationalist zones are considerable.

D. Psychological Warfare against French Union Forces.

In the case of propaganda directed against the armed forces of the French and Vietnam nationalist troops, the propaganda services of the Democratic Republic take into full account the ethnic and national differences between the various component units of the French Union Forces. There exists a "tactical" propaganda specifically designed to influence the units immediately concerned so as to reduce their combat effectiveness; and a "strategic," long-range propaganda designed to incite the individuals subjected to it to become propagandists for the Communist cause upon their return to their homelands. In the latter case, there are special leaflets designed for the major ethnic groups, e.g., the Moroccans, Senegalese, Algerians, Metropolitan French, etc.

European communist parties also actively intervene in this propaganda war. Thus, the French Communist Party distributes leaflets and books to seamen (41) aboard Indochina-bound ships, and the East-German "Social Unity Party" also distributes German-language leaflets in the name of the German Democratic Government to Foreign Legionnaires of German origin. Such leaflets reach the territory of the D.R.V.N. from China and are then distributed by the Dich-Van in the garrison areas.

For example, a leaflet, printed in Arabic for the Moroccan troops, read in part:

Moroccan soldiers,
    You fight for an unjust cause at the service of your oppressors.
...The Americans and the French carve up your country. Moroccan

soldiers, the Vietnamese are your brothers...the soldiers of the
Vietnamese Army fight against your oppressors for the liberty and
independence of their country... (42)

A similar leaflet in the name of the East-German Soviet-sponsored government reads:

The Government of the German Democratic Republic appeals to all Germans
who have been impressed into the French colonial army as Foreign
Legionnaires to cease that dirty and criminal war against Vietnam and
to come over to the Vietnam People's Army...thus they shall not only
save their lives, but also the honor of the German Nation... The
Government of the German Democratic Republic guarantees to all German
soldiers who...come over to the Vietnam People's Army, a full amnesty,
work according to their wishes and ability, and possibilities for
professional training /and/ will do its utmost to facilitate the
return home of those German soldiers. (43)

Such appeals have a certain amount of success, and over the past two years,
several transports of former German Foreign Legionnaires have been repatriated
to East Germany via People's China and the Soviet Union. Similar convoys of
nationals of what is now the People's Democracies of Poland, Czechoslovakia and
Rumania, have also been repatriated to their countries of origin. It is to be
seriously questioned whether the latter prisoners returned to their former
homelands upon their own free will, and no neutral commission ever investigated
the legality of such repatriations (44).

It is noteworthy that throughout the whole duration of the war, the
authorities of the Democratic Republic have continued to repatriate French
civilian and military prisoners in small numbers by simply arranging for a
local cease-fire, or by merely letting the liberated prisoners walk towards
the French lines.

E. Indoctrination of Prisoners of War.

The treatment given French Union prisoners of war is similar to that given
United Nations prisoners in Korea by the Chinese and Korean People's Forces, and,
therefore, includes ideological indoctrination as well as working as coolies to
haul military supplies for their captors (45).

Thus, the 297 French Union prisoners (Europeans and Africans) released
under a Christmas amnesty in December, 1953, addressed the following appeal to
their comrades in the French Expeditionary Corps:

...The lenient measure taken in our favour by the Government of the
Democratic Republic of Vietnam, is an expression of the policy of a
mighty state... The Vietnamese people -- whose victorious army is
invincible -- fight on till complete liberation of their country and
total annihilation of the colonialist aggressors.

The French people have realised that peace in Vietnam has become a
national need for France to safeguard her independence ravished by the
U.S. imperialists... In the French colonies in Africa, more and more
numerous people have arised (sic) to fight for national independence
and to put an end to colonialist exploitation and repression...

The Government of the Democratic Republic of Vietnam-- the sole Government which has released its POWs when war is still raging on its territory-- undertakes to awaken, THROUGH CORRECT AND CONVINCING EXPLANATIONS, the men deceived by the propaganda of the French colonialists, lackeys of the American imperialists...

Let this International Day of struggle be an opportunity for the whole French Expeditionary Corps to take part in the building of peace in Vietnam and the world!...

Long live President Ho Chi Minh! (46)

In many aspects, the above declaration even outdoes the work carried out by the North Korean and Chinese propagandists, and makes the repatriation particularly of the African prisoners an extremely complicated problem. A strong protest against such an "inadmissible political indoctrination of the prisoners" was radioed to the Viet-Minh command by the French Government on January 15, 1954, but it is doubtful that it will bring any results (47).

While germ warfare charges have not been preferred on a large scale (although the French are held responsible for every epidemic or crop plague occurring in the territory under control of the Republic) French pilots are subject to a particularly thorough "convincing explanation" and are being used to broadcast appeals to their fellow-pilots in the French Far Eastern Air Force:

...For 17 months I had fought against this people which I did not even know. If people asked me the reason why I came to Indochina, and why France has been waging the war in this country, I would feel...ashamed of my ignorance.

...As for us, what are we fighting for? We are fighting for a handful of French capitalists and for American imperialists who, forced to sign an armistice in Korea, are compelling the French rulers to drag on this war...with the blood of French soldiers.

Comrade pilots, we should no longer fight against the Vietnamese people...we must fight for the cessation of this dirty way through repatriation of the French Expeditionary Corps and immediate negotiations with the VN People's Government headed by President Ho Chi Minh. (48)

In fact, the indoctrination of the prisoners of war does not cease with their release and repatriation to France. In France itself, the French Communist Party intermittently prints a newspaper, the Voix du Rapatrié (49), allegedly written by former prisoners, which keeps the repatriate informed on developments in the Democratic Republic even though he has returned to civilian life. Likewise, the families of prisoners who have died while in captivity receive letters of condolence from the Republican Government, posted in Czechoslovakia by a so-called "French-Vietnamese Friendship Association." Such a thorough "follow-up" of each individual case constitutes a rather unique example of the possibilities of unlimited psychological warfare.

4. Foreign Relations.

While the foreign relations of a country are generally part of the governmental process, the conduct of foreign relations in the D.R.V.N. -- mainly in view of the present war situation-- has remained first and foremost a political prerogative of the Workers' Party.

Formal relations between the Democratic Republic and foreign powers began in 1950, when the Chinese People's Republic recognized the D.R.V.N. on January 18, to be followed by the Soviet Union on January 31, and by the various Eastern European satellite nations during the following months. Yugoslavia has recognized the Ho Chi Minh regime but was refused recognition by the latter, in view of Marshal Tito's break with the Kominform bloc.

The Republic has only two embassies abroad: in Moscow, headed by Nguyen Luong Bang; and one in Paking, under Hoang Van Hoan. The latter, furthermore, has a large information staff. It is not known whether anyone of the Soviet bloc countries maintains a full-fledged diplomatic mission within Vietnam (50). Military missions, however, are maintained by both the Soviet Union and People's China. No international treaties signed by the Republican Government have come to light thus far, with the possible exception of a military assistance pact allegedly signed by Ho during his visit to Peiping in the spring of 1950. More recently, on March 28, 1954, according to a U.P. despatch from Taipeh (51), an eight-power committee (U.S.S.R., People's China, Czechoslovakia, Poland, East Germany, Hungary, Rumania, Bulgaria) was allegedly set up at Peiping to procure aid to the amount of $500 million a year for the D.R.V.N., with the Soviet Union donating one-half of the sum in equipment, China $150 million, and the remainder to be split up among the other member governments.

However, the most important development in the D.R.V.N.'s foreign relations is the appearance of a full-fledged delegation of the Viet-Minh regime at the Geneva Peace Conference on Korea and Indochina, which began on April 26, 1954. Pham Van Dong, the Vice-President of the D.R.V.N. and a long-term member of the ICP, was made "Special Minister of Foreign Affairs" and head of the Democratic Republic's delegation to Geneva, instead of Hoang Minh Giam, the regular Minister of Foreign Affairs, who is a Socialist. Nguyen Luong Bang, the Republic's ambassador to Peking, is his deputy, and the third member of the delegation appears to be Phan Anh, a former Socialist minister of one of Ho's earlier cabinet combinations. Hence, it can be safely assumed that no "deviationism" may be expected from the D.R.V.N. delegation to the conference.

The Workers' Party also maintains an extensive network of missions abroad, and has sent delegations to most of the more important international conferences recently held by Communist organizations: peace congresses at Vienna, Austria; youth festivals in Berlin and Bucharest; and other congresses of women, students, journalists, labor organizations, etc., in other countries of the Soviet orbit. Other permanent non-diplomatic missions are maintained in various parts of Southeast Asia. One such is the Vietnam News Service in Rangoon, Burma, which distributes literature and news bulletins emanating from the D.R.V.N., but which also serves, as will be seen later, as an unofficial intermediary between the Viet-Minh and Western emissaries. There is also some evidence that in the recent past the Viet-Minh or later Workers' Party made a serious attempt to assume the leadership of the other Communist-inspired "national liberation movements" in Thailand, Burma and Malaya -- not to speak of those of Cambodia and Laos which are totally under the Party's control. Three Viet-Minh or Party sponsored organizations were successively set up to achieve this goal: the Southeast Asia League, which collapsed in 1948 after a brief open appearance in Thailand prior to Marshal Phibun's return to power, and which was led by a Moscow-trained Vietnamese, Tran Van Giau; the Ku Sap Be (52), which operated under Nguyen Van Long, another Moscow-trained Vietnamese; and lastly, the Communist Co-Ordination Committee

for Southeast Asia, at Muong Lene (or Monghlen) in the Southern Shan States,
Burma, which -- as its name implies -- supposedly coordinates the operations
of the Communist parties on the whole Southeast Asian mainland (53) and
Indonesia. Nguyen Van Long, the former leader of the now defunct Ku Sap Be,
is the present head of the Co-Ordination Committee, which comprises a
council of two Red Chinese, two Malayan Chinese, two Vietnamese, two Burmese,
two Thai, two Lao, two Indonesians and one Cambodian (54). There also seem
to be connections between the China-sponsored "Free Thai" state and the Co-
Ordination Committee.

While it seems unlikely that China (or the Soviet Union, for that matter)
has relinquished an overall direction of communist political influence in the
area to the Republic, the latter appears to have a not uncertain amount of
influence over the lesser developed and smaller revolutionary parties in
Southeast Asia. It is also likely that such a Vietnamese-directed "co-operation"
would meet with less resistance than if the operation were openly under Chinese
control.

Attempts have been made by the Republican government to "break out" of
the relatively narrow circle of its present allies by seeking recognition
among the neutral and anti-colonialist Asian nations. Two missions were sent
to India in 1950; one in July under Mai The Chau (now first secretary at the
D.R.V.N. Embassy at Peking), and one other as a private mission from Ho Chi
Minh to Premier Nehru, under Nguyen Minh (now also in Peking as head of the
information bureau), in October, 1950. Both failed to gain recognition
(but so did the Bao Dai government), and similar attempts in Burma, Indonesia
and Thailand have met a like fate. Still, in the latter country, the Viet-Minh
operates quite openly and still maintains a procurement commission, a local
propaganda office, and a Vietnam Emigrant Association. All newspapers in the
Vietnamese language have ceased publication in Thailand, however. Mr. Le Trung
still publishes a Thai-language periodical which is smuggled into Laos via
the northeastern Thai border provinces. An unofficial delegation headed by
Hoang Quoc Viet and Ton Duc Thang, also visited the Korean People's Republic
in 1952.

There are no officially known Republican emissaries in Hong Kong and
Singapore, with the exception of the People's Army procurement commissions
which operate there. Viet-Minh propaganda there is distributed -- as throughout the British Empire -- by the local People's China or Communist bookstore.

The Republic has succeeded in implanting Workers' Party cells among the
strong Vietnamese minority groups in various parts of the French Union.
Such cells are known to exist in New Caledonia and the New Hebrides as well
as in British and French Guiana, where the action is directed by the Vietnam
Emigrant Association.

In France itself, constitutional guarantees forbid the imprisonment of
a known Vietnamese (or any) member of the Communist Party, so long as his
actions do not openly affect French national security. This situation led
to the paradoxical fact that while France was fighting a war with the D.R.V.N.
in Indochina, the latter's representatives in France continued to publish
anti-French literature and to maintain a fully-staffed mission. The mission
was closed in 1949, along with most of the open activities of the Vietnam
Republican Government. Tran Ngoc Dan, the chief of the Republican mission
in France was arrested, but soon replaced by Pham Huy Thong, a member of long

standing of the French Communist Party (55), who reconstituted the Viet-Minh's network in France on an underground basis to a point of efficiency which led him to declare publicly in Bordeaux on December 24, 1951:

> Our movement is now organized clandestinely. New repressive measures of the French Government could not harm us.

The efficiency of the Vietnam Republic's intelligence service in France can be judged by the fact that in 1950 it succeeded in obtaining copies of the top-secret Revers Rapport (56) which soon found its way to General Vo Nguyen Giap, and resulted in the dismissal of the then Chief of the French General Staff.

It now appears, however, that there still exist intermittent contacts between non-Communist French legislators and the Viet-Minh. On March 12, 1954, Mr. Raphaël Leygues, Member of the French Union Assembly, stated in the parliamentary record that he undertook, in 1953, a mission of information to Rangoon, Burma, in order to contact plenipotentiaries of the Republican Government in order to investigate the possibilities of direct "useful negotiations" between France and the D.R.V.N. (57)

It is even more remarkable that this mission had been undertaken at the behest of Mr. Vincent Auriol, then President of the French Republic, and

> with the active sympathy of Messrs. Robert Schuman, Queuille and Pleven. Mr. Jean Letourneau /then Minister for the Associated States7 gave us his explicit approval...
>
> We have seen that the Viet-Minh -- while in favor of such contacts -- wanted to talk to responsible persons. (58)

It is not yet known whether other such missions have taken place under similar circumstances after the breakdown of Mr. Paul Mus' mission in 1947 (59). The Leygues mission to Rangoon is also interesting in view of the fact that Leygues' only companion was a Vietnamese scientist of world-wide reputation in the field of radiology: Mr. Buu-Hoi -- a relative of Prince Buu-Loc, premier of the Vietnam National Government. One may, therefore, safely assume that the conversations took place with the full knowledge of Vietnamese nationalist circles (60), the more so as the D.R.V.N. radio referred to them publicly in several of its broadcasts.

According to Mr. Leygues, the conversations were finally sabotaged by an unnamed "well-known personality"; news of the existence of such conversations were then suppressed by order of Letourneau, and Leygues came to the conclusion that the failure of the mission was imputable

> ...more to lethargy rather than bad intention...I have come to the disheartening conclusion that there is a collusion in immobilism and inertia between the 'diehards' among the Viet-Minh and the 'softies' among the French. (61)

With the establishment in 1949 of a High Commission of the Vietnam National Government in France, the struggle began in earnest for the allegiance of the 40-odd thousand Vietnamese who reside in France, particularly within the many student and welfare organizations which include most of these Vietnamese. A series of political murders (nearly all unsolved, of course) of Vietnamese

residents occurred, and despite a now sharply-increasing counter-propaganda
and police surveillance, the situation still falls short of being clearly in
favor of the Vietnam National Government.

Britain's Vietnamese residents are mostly organized as a subsidiary of
larger organizations in France. Republican propaganda and literature is
distributed there by the Hsinhua (New China) News Agency.

In the European satellite countries, there are small groups of Vietnamese
students attending universities in Poland, Czechoslovakia, East Berlin and
in the Soviet Union. They are under the jurisdiction of their embassy in
Moscow. In the United States, the Vietnam Republican point of view was expounded by the Vietnam-American Friendship Association (V.A.F.A.), created in
1945 in Hanoi by a group of Vietnamese with the help of the local OSS mission
of Major General Gallagher and Major Patti. It published a bulletin, the
V.A.F.A. Review, in both English and Vietnamese, and for a while operated an
office in New York City at 796 Ninth Avenue.

A. Relations with the other Indochinese States.

The relations between the Democratic Republic of Vietnam and its two
brother-states of Cambodia and Laos offer a certain amount of interest inasmuch
as in their case the D.R.V.N. seeks to ally its Marxist ideology with the
purely Vietnamese-nationalistic aim of expansion at the expense of the two
weaker, less-developed and thinly-populated areas. Of the two again, it is
Laos which is the most backward, so that its "People's Democratic" development
is at its most rudimentary beginnings. It is for that reason that the development of the relations between the D.R.V.N. and Cambodia might be taken as an
adequate yardstick of the eventual development of Vietnam-Khmer relations,
should the D.R.V.N. gain control of the whole Vietnamese territory.

In the early postwar days, Cambodia and Laos had had their own national
awakenings which, on the whole, had remained nationalistic. In Laos, a die-
hard group of completely insignificant strength gathered around Prince
Souphanu Vong and with him joined the Viet-Minh. During the Spring offensive
of 1953, the Viet-Minh established Souphanu Vong in Samneua (Laos) as the
head of a "Free Laotian Government."

Vietnam has a more direct interest in Cambodia inasmuch as the latter
has been Vietnam's favorite overflow area for the last 150 years. All of
South Vietnam is in fact a group of former Khmer provinces, and French
intervention in the 1860's, by "freezing" the Khmer-Vietnamese border,
probably saved Cambodia from an early annexation and assimilation by the more
powerful neighboring state (62). However, France's integration of the three
states into the Indochinese Federation brought about one unexpected result:
it brought many Vietnamese into positions of responsibility in the territories
of the two other states. Vietnamese were engineers, doctors, civil service
officials and administrators; and the same trend of development was reflected
in the illegal politics of the prewar era, where practically all command
posts of the old ICP were in Vietnamese hands. Thus, in 1945, an individual
of mixed Vietnamese-Khmer descent, Son Ngoc Thanh, after a colorful career
as a Japanese captain, seized temporary control of the Khmer capital in the
name of a Free Khmer (Khmer Issara) Government. Soon captured by the French
and released in 1951, he re-entered Cambodia and joined the Viet-Minh which,
in the absence of any marked Cambodian personality, had in the meantime

gained nearly full control of the Khmer Issara movement. The infiltration
of the Cambodian Liberation Movement by the Democratic Republic of Vietnam
is a classroom example of a bloodless "revolution from within."

The Workers' Party and the Khmer Issara.

It began in 1949 by the creation of a "Canvassing Committee for the Creation
of a Revolutionary Cambodian People's Party" (Ban Van Dong Thanh Lap Dang Nhan
Cach Mang Cao Mien), almost entirely composed of carefully-selected Vietnamese
with considerable experience in Khmer affairs. In conformity with the old
Komintern directive to unite first of all the "activity of the various national
revolutionary organizations..." (63), the Committee's action was at first
entirely limited to promulgating simple Khmer-nationalist slogans:

> Cambodia's independence is not real since the French are still here...
> The lack of security is due to the fact that the French are still
> here. Let the French go and security will return immediately... The
> Viet-Minh will leave as soon as /Khmer/ independence is attained... (64)

The next step was the creation of special Vietnamese armed units under
the command of the South Vietnam inter-zone, known as "Vietnam Troops to Help
Cambodia." Such units completely took over what became the "Southwestern Zone"
(Kampot and Kompong Speu) and soon the whole South Vietnam Zone Command of
the Vietnam People's Army transferred its headquarters to Preyveng Province
in Cambodia, finding it quieter than tightly-controlled South Vietnam; these
were followed by the "Central Office South" (65), and the bulk of the Viet-Minh's
regional commands. The "Central Office South" was headed by Sieu Heng, again
a revolutionary of mixed Khmer-Vietnamese ancestry.

In 1950 began the installation of a complete network of "Cadre Committees"
(Ban Can Su) under the overall direction of a Vietnamese, Nguyen Than Son, using
the Cambodian alias of Hanilakiri. Cambodia was split into three zones
(mien); several sectors (vung); and numerous local units (srok, khum, phum).
At zone level, the Ban Can Su Southwest had no Cambodian members, while the
two other zone committees had one Cambodian member each out of seven members
on each committee. Inter-cell branches (lien-chi) and cells were set up
just as on Vietnamese soil.

In the meantime, the "Canvassing Committees" had not remained idle and
had blossomed out into the Khmer equivalent of UBKC/HCs. For example, the
committee for the Phnom-Penh area is composed as follows:

a. Ban Can Su - for executive and overall leadership;

b. To Khiem Soat Thanh - the City Control Cell in charge of security
   and counter-intelligence;

c. Ban Giao Thong Lien Lac - the Liaison and Communications Committee
   with two sub-cells for
   1. Liaison with the "liberated" zone (i.e., Viet-Minh-held
      territory);
   2. Liaison with the "temporarily-occupied" (i.e., French Union-
      controlled) areas;

d. Ban Tuyen Huan - in charge of cadre training, printing and
   distributing of propaganda;

e. <u>Chi Quan Bao Thanh</u> - Military Security Committee;

f. <u>Ban Hoa Van Than Thien</u> - Chinese Cultural and Friendship Committee.

With the creation of the Lao Dong Party in 1951, the Democratic Republic now possessed the adequate political tool to create a brother-revolutionary party -- making due allowance, of course, for the lack of political sophistication of the Cambodian masses. This new party, the <u>Dang Nhan Dan Cach Mang Cao Mien</u> ("Revolutionary Cambodian People's Party") was not only entirely created by the Lao Dong, but its very name and statutes had to be <u>translated</u> from Vietnamese into Cambodian! A covering letter addressed by the <u>Central Intervention Committee</u> to its zonal branches is most revealing in the matter:

To all Comrades -

Enclosed are two documents concerning:
1. the Statute of the Revolutionary Cambodian People's Party (66);
2. the political platform of the Party.

The statute has been unanimously approved by the <u>Ban Can Su</u> of Cambodia. As far as the platform is concerned, it has only approved the general ideas which you shall use as a basis in your canvassing and instructing the new adherents of the R.C.P.P....

We request the zones to have it translated into Khmer and to have it circulated only within the organizations. We hope that during the period of canvassing and recruiting of adherents and the constitution of <u>Chi-bo</u> /cells/...you will complete the present document with your opinions which you will transmit to the Central Intervention Committee before Feburary, 1952.

The Central Intervention Committee then shall centralize all the opinion and inspire itself therefrom to elaborate the Official Political Credo of the Party which then will be officially distributed among the people once it has been approved by the <u>Ban Can Su</u> for Cambodia. (67)

The final statute of the R.C.P.P. as it emerged from the discussions of the three zonal commands resembles a very simplified version of the statutes of the Lao Dong, with one major difference: <u>nowhere</u> in the whole text can one find a reference to the "great teachers" of the Marxist doctrine, and the only mention of political shading is contained in the guarded sentence: "The doctrine of the Party is the doctrine of Popular Democracy" (68).

In 1951, Sieu Heng, already head of the "Central Office South," also became president of the "Cambodian National Liberation Committee," the pseudo-government of the Khmer revolutionaries. One year later again, the "Cambodian National Liberation Committee" went one step further. A "Cambodian Resistance Government" was set up under Son Ngoc Thanh, now known as Son Ngoc Minh, which was promptly recognized by the D.R.V.N. and the "Free Laotian Government" -- but by no one else.

Recently, the interest of the Viet-Minh in Cambodia has become more apparent. French stations monitoring Viet-Minh radio broadcasts reported a series of lengthy reports on Cambodian affairs by a visiting Viet-Minh mission, composed, among others, of Tran Van Nguyen, a member of the UBKC/HC Nam-Bo; Bui Van Bu, a delegate of the Lien-Viet Front of Nam-Bo; as well as of two "Cambodian National Combatants, Enemy-Exterminators," Duong Nghia and Ly Ngay (whose Cambodian nationality seems of recent date, considering their Vietnamese names).

The avowed aim of that inspection mission was "to visit President Son Ngo Minh; the combatants and the populations of a friendly country as well as the Chinese nationals.../and/ also to see the Vietnamese civilians and soldiers residing in Cambodia." (69)

> The conferences which we held and the information which we gave... have reinforced the confidence of the Cambodian people in the victorious power of the Republic of Vietnam, of Cambodia, Laos, and of the World Camp of Peace and Democracy directed by the Soviet Union.

That a large-scale "Gleichschaltung" has taken place between the Viet-Minh and the Cambodian revolutionaries is further apparent in a statement by Kemoni, the "Foreign Minister of the Cambodian Resistance Government," of March 20, 1954, in which he violently protests against "the American intervention in Indochina":

> In view of the increasing development of the Cambodian Liberation War, the American imperialists intervene more and more in Cambodia. Furthermore, the American interventionists pull the wires behind the puppet /King/ Sihanouk to make him play the farce of independence so as to evict, little by little, the French and to directly take over the war. (70)

The young Democratic Republic of Vietnam had learned its lesson well. Hardly five years after its own liberation from the chains of colonialism, and in the midst of a war for its own survival, it had created a full-fledged satellite of its own.

The outlook is hardly more brilliant for Prince Souphanu Vong's Pathet Lao government at Samneua. In Laos' case, too, a Dang Lao Doc Lap (Vietnamese for "Lao Independence Party") was created by the Lao Dong and nearly entirely staffed by Vietnamese. Administratively, the D.R.V.N. treats Laos as an occupied area and has established three regional "Delegates for Political Liaison of the Front" (Phai Vien Lien Lac Chinh-tri Tran va Dia Phuong). From what is known through the evaluation of captured documents, one arrives at the following overall picture of future relations of the D.R.V.N. with its two "younger brother" states:

1. Satellization of the two states;

2. Outright annexation of certain provinces already now given a Vietnamese provincial administration, as is the case of the "Inter-Provinces" of Phong Saly -- Sam Neua, Luang Prabang -- Huei-Sai; and Tranninh, in Laos; and the Southwestern Zone in Cambodia. (See Map II.)

The results thus achieved by the Democratic Republic are in full accordance with Vietnam's traditional aims and will undoubtedly greatly contribute in establishing Vietnam's eventual hegemony over the Southeast Asian peninsula, for -- if in any sense victorious in the present war -- it will be the strongest military power from the hills of Kwangsi to those of the Arakan.

B. The Workers' Party and the Non-Vietnamese Minorities.

The problem of ethnic minorities is one of the most crucial which any
Vietnamese government has to face. While Vietnam's population is overwhelmingly
Vietnamese, this majority's occupancy of the country is practically limited
to the rice-growing flatlands and to the larger of the mountain cities. At
least three-fifths of the territory are occupied by such minorities as the
Thai, Muong, Man, Tho and Nung in the north; and by such aboriginal hill
tribes as the Rhadé, Hré, Jarai, and Bahnar, living in the South Annam jungle
plateaux. Another strong minority is constituted by the Khmer ethnic
islands in South Vietnam, which amount to about 400,000. However, the most
important group both from the economic and political point of view is made
up of about a million and a half Chinese and additional thousands of Minh-
Huong (half-bloods of mixed Sino-Vietnamese ancestry) who permanently reside
in Vietnam (71).

The Chinese.

Grouped into solidly-entrenched "congregations" around the major
population centers, the Chinese control a good share of the overall commerce
of the country and have a nearly complete stranglehold over the rice industry.
As throughout the rest of Southeast Asia, they also constitute the majority
of the money lenders in the country, and—— along with some of the bigger
French firms and banking institutions—— control the bulk of the fluid capital
available.

In view of Vietnam's century-old position as a tributary or semi-
dependency of the Chinese Empire, the Chinese have succeeded in the past in
obtaining for their congregations a statute of administrative semi-autonomy
which the French have preserved (and which, in fact, they were forced to
extend even further under the 1946 Sino-French Agreement (72)) and which the
Vietnam National Government has thus far respected. The D.R.V.N. was
painfully made aware of the existence of the Chinese problem during its
first years of existence (see Part I) and now appears to have concentrated
its efforts upon integrating the Chinese minority into the overall political
structure of the country. As shown on pages 38-39, the Lao Dong has assured

> citizens of the People's Democracies, particularly the Overseas Chinese,
> that they may enjoy the same rights and fulfill the same duties as the
> Vietnamese citizens if such is their desire and if they have the
> approval of their country and of the Vietnamese government...

Three major organizations were created by the Republican Government to
cope with the problem of the Overseas Chinese. These were the

a. Chinese Canvassing Committee, or Ban Hoa Van Trung Uong, under
   the General Directorate of Political Affairs of the Ministry of
   National Defense;

b. Chinese Affairs Committee, or Ban Hue Kieu Vu, a mixed body which
   may be found at all administrative levels;

c. the Vietnam-Chinese Friendship Association, which promotes good
   will between the two peoples, and is a member of the Lien-Viet
   Front. It even operates an office in Thailand.

As we have seen previously (p. 55), the Ban Can Su in Cambodia and Laos also has a Chinese Liaison Committee (Ban Hoa Van Thang) to co-ordinate Viet-Minh activities with the local Chinese "congregations." On the other hand, the Chinese Communist Party operates its own network in Indochina independently of the local Communist organization, and has done so for over twenty years. Secondly, the Overseas Chinese are kept "in line" by pressure and terror exercised by local delegates of the "Overseas Chinese Commission," directed by Mme. Ho Shiang Ying of Swatow. Thus, in its own way, People's China has maintained the almost "extraterritorial" status of the Chinese nationals in Indochina, although the latter are still represented-- for the time being-- by a Consul-General of the Taipeh government.

Chinese participation (73) in the Indochina war-- contrary to that in Malaya-- is mostly limited to financial contributions which are paid by nearly all Chinese, whether they reside in territory under control of the Republican Government or not. Such efforts are co-ordinated by the "South Vietnam Overseas Chinese Liberation League," created in 1950. The report of the League for the year 1951-52 emphasizes that it had

> ...made collections and donated to the Vietnam People's Army large quantities of hand-grenades and other weapons, donated land to the Vietnam People's Government, etc. Many Chinese youths...joined the Vietnam People's Army...meanwhile, Chinese residents living in French-occupied towns and areas participated in the Vietnam people's struggles against forced conscription... All activities of Chinese residents in South Vietnam this year will follow the slogan: 'Unite with the Vietnam People and oppose the French and American imperialists and the Chiang Kai Shek lackeys so as to liberate Vietnam and defend China. (74)

Still, the Republican Government seems to have the same difficulties overcoming the natural distrust of the Vietnamese for their mighty neighbor to the north, and "spontaneous" demonstrations of Sino-Vietnamese friendship always take on a somewhat strained air, in spite of their rather elaborate preparation, as was the case during last year's celebrations of People's China's national holiday on October 1, 1953-- an official holiday in the Democratic Republic.

> B. Solemn ceremonies should be organized in all localities where conditions permit it, regardless of whether there are any Chinese present or not.

> C. 1. Write to the Vietnam-China Friendship Association which will edit in due time a booklet containing an interesting documentation on New China.

> 2. The Party cadres at every level will have all members...study this booklet. They then will send propagandists to the villages, hamlets and communities where they will constitute cells which will be able to inform the population and...exalt the feeling of solidarity which animates the Vietnamese and Chinese peoples.

> 3. ...The responsible cadres will exercise strict control over all these manifestations and will send us their reports as soon as possible. We must be able to learn from the experience as soon as possible, so as to reinforce propaganda efficiency among the civilian services and the military units... (75)

The test of the lessons thus learned came in the period between January 18 and February 18, 1954, which was named "Vietnam-Soviet-Friendship Month" and was marked by a long speech by Ton Duc Thang, President of the Lien-Viet and also President of the National Committee for Vietnam-Soviet Friendship, exalting the bonds of friendship existing between the three nations (76). However, the expected results apparently failed to materialize, for "...after a couple of days it got relatively little attention even on the Communist radio" (77). Still, there can be no doubt as to the fact that in view of the Republic's dependence upon China-channeled Soviet Aid, increasingly close relations with People's China will continue to prevail, even though these may bring about a progressive control of Vietnamese affairs by its northern neighbor-- in the old tradition which existed long before the arrival of both the French and Marxism.

Other Ethnic Minorities.

While both the Republic's Constitution of 1946 and the Workers' Party Platform proclaim the complete equality of the various ethnic minorities with the Vietnamese, it is inevitable that the Vietnamese element will eventually hold a preponderant position in the affairs of these minorities, all promises to the contrary notwithstanding.

In general, the creation of a Workers' Party cell network in the territory of an ethnic minority presents the same problems as the creation of Khmer or Lao parties. Also, as in the case of the Vietnamese relations with the Chinese, there is a basic repugnance on the part of the mountain tribes, particularly the Tho and Thai, to control by the "peoples from the plains," i.e., the Vietnamese whom they consider as foreigners (78). This is clearly reflected in the minutes of a cadre conference held in 1953 at Son-La (Thai Territory) by the Provincial Executive Committee of the DLD:

> 1. The population mistrusts us in a certain measure, in view of the numerous false words of our can-bo...
> The can-bo from the Delta (79) do not know the language of the region; there are so many dialects.
> There is a lack of propaganda documents /in the local dialects/ thus wasting a great deal of time. (80)

In other areas such as the Upper Tonking Region inhabited by the Tho minority, under Viet-Minh control over an extended period, the Republic's integration program of the local minorities has made better headway. Congresses are held for the benefit of the minorities, and at least one member of the Tho minority has attained rank and fame in the Republican Government: General Chu Van Tan, a member of the Central Executive Committee of the DLD, and Chairman of the UBKC/HC of the vital Viet-Bac Inter-zone, which contains the major depots of the People's Army and also houses Ho Chi Minh and the whole Republican Government (81). The last known conference of minority leaders took place from August 30 to September 10, 1953, precisely under the chairmanship of Chu Van Tan. More than 140 delegates from 20 minority groups attended

> ...side-by-side with emulation fighters elected among the guerilla farmers and workers of the war services... (82)

In his address to the delegates, Chu Van Tan pointed out the progress achieved by the minorities under the guidance of the Republican Government and stated its aim as uniting "the brother peoples of the Viet-Bac region in order to study the policy of the Government." At the end of the conference, the delegates

> unanimously voted a motion denouncing the maneuvers of the French imperialists and...expressing the will of the delegates to support to the hilt the policy of the Lao Dong Party, of the People's Government and of the Lien Viet Front. (82)

Still, the battle for the loyalties of the mountain tribes is far from won for the Republican Government. As a matter of fact, the Lao Dong Party reports from the Lao-Kay and Son-La area that the population aids and informs units of the French-led Groupe Commando Mixte Authochtone (83) operating deeply behind Viet-Minh lines while it does not accord similar help to the People's Army.

The "Thai Free State".

Little can be said about a new buffer state which the Chinese Central People's Government sponsors in the South Yunnan watershed area, proclaiming its existence on July 24, 1953. It purports to have created an autonomous Thai state for all the Thai tribes in the area, and would include the Sip Song Chau T'ai -- the twelve Thai "baronies" -- on the Vietnam side of the Yunnan border and the four Thai "baronies" located in Yunnan, as well as the Chingpo or Kachin tribes of the China-Burma border region.

The new "government," presided over by the Tai Tao Chin O Pan, supposedly has seven vice-presidents of whom three are Chingpo and three are Thai. Presumably, the seventh is either a member of one of the other minority tribes (Huni, Nang, etc.), or Chinese. The legislative assembly has 385 members. (84)

With the loss of the Thai capital of Lai-Chau to the Democratic Republic during the winter campaign of 1953-54, the problem which such a Thai state might create -- astride the whole watershed area from Burma through Thailand and Laos -- has become more acute, the more so as Mao Tse-tung apparently has relinquished to Ho Chi Minh the administrative control of the Thai territories situated in Yunnan (85) in order to unify the area under one single control authority. Only time will tell whether the new state, under Sino-Vietnamese sponsorship, will be able to create a pole of attraction for Thai or other discontented segments of the Southeast Asian peninsula.

5. Religion in the Republic.

From the religious point of view, Vietnam represents one of the more curious mosaics in its part of the world: 80% of the population is nominally Buddhist, but not with the emphasis or religious fervor displayed in other parts of Southeast Asia. Another 10% of the population is Catholic, while the remaining 10% belongs to the two major politico-religious sects of the Cao-Dai and the Hoa-Hao, or practises primitive animism (the southern aboriginal tribes), or has been converted to Protestantism by missionaries. Oddly enough, religion has presented no barrier to Communism in Indochina. On the contrary, in view of the evidence at hand it is possible to affirm that it was the Catholic church of Indochina which has given to the Republican Government much of its erstwhile international credit (86).

Buddhism never presented much of a political problem to the Democratic Republic. It soon developed a type of "National Buddhism" (Tinh Doc Cu Si) patterned upon the "National Churches" existing in the U.S.S.R. and Eastern Europe. The head bonze is Tien Chieu, known to be a member of the ICP. In North Vietnam, a Buddhist "National Salvation" Sect (Hoi Phat Giao Cu'u Quoc) flourishes under Nguyen The Long, a member of the National Committee of the Lien Viet Front. The southern feudal politico-religious sects proved to be a tougher nut to crack, since they aspired to share in the temporal power of the state. In their case, the Viet-Minh attempted outright force. Huyn Phu So, the "Mad Bonze" and head of the Hoa-Hao sect, was executed for rebellion on May 20, 1947, and the Viet-Minh began a Saint-Bartholomew of the Hoa-Hao followers.

A similar attempt upon the Cao-Dai and their stronghold at Tayninh also met with failure and both sects have become more or less willing allies of the Franco-Vietnamese Nationalist forces. Occasional desertions -- such as those of Ba-Cut, who switched from the nationalist side to the "attentist" side several times in the past few years -- are due more to interference of the National Government with what the sects consider as their feudal prerogatives than to a change of heart on the part of the sect members.

This leaves the Catholics as the only sizeable religious force whose weight in favor of one of the adversaries might affect the balance of power as it exists now in Indochina.

The Viet-Minh and the Catholics.

There.can be no doubt as to the fact that the Catholic Church of Indochina stood in the forefront of Vietnamese nationalism during its early days, and in so doing received the wholehearted support of the French Catholic Church. There is also no doubt that the Catholic Church of Vietnam merely expressed the deep feelings of its members. The best example is that of Empress Nam Phuong, wife of Bao Dai, herself a very devout Catholic from South Vietnam. On the very day of her husband's abdication, she sent the following message to her many friends abroad:

> Vietnam has liberated itself from the yoke of the French and Japanese imperialists. In abdicating, my husband, the ex-emperor Bao Dai has proclaimed his preference to be a simple citizen of a free country rather than king of a vassalized one. I myself have abandoned without regret my prerogatives of empress in order to unite myself with my sister to help our Government -- each one according to her abilities -- to defend the sacred cause of our independence.

> Blood flows abundantly at the present moment...many human lives are offered in holocaust to the ambition and cupidity of a group of French colonialists...

> In the name of 13 million women of Vietnam, I ask my personal friends, the friends of Vietnam, to raise their voices to claim the freedom and right... Asking that your respective governments intervene so as to establish a just and equitable peace you will have obeyed an overriding duty to humanity and won the thankfulness of our whole people.

> (s) Mme. Vinh Thuy
> Ex-Empress Nam Phuong (87)

This appeal, written on August 25, 1945, was soon followed by an official appeal of the four Vietnamese Bishops to Pope Pius XII on September 23, 1945, while Ho Chi Minh's government was still struggling for the control of the Red River Delta:

> Our dear people of Annam has wanted to take advantage of the intercession of its four Bishops to offer to Your Holiness the homage of its profound respect and to implore the benediction...of Your Holiness in favor of our independence... We Annamite Bishops beg Your Holiness, the Court of Rome, their Eminencies the Cardinals, their Excellencies the Archbishops, the Bishops and all the Catholics of the whole Universe and especially those of France, to support the decision of our dear Fatherland. (88)

Indeed, the Catholics fought very well on the side of the Republican Government during the first years of the struggle, and the role of the Vietnamese Catholics was described as follows in a Catholic review:

> The whole Annamite Christendom, with its fifteen hundred priests and two million faithful, has not hesitated to follow the example of its bishops ...There is no need of other proofs but the spontaneous attitude of the Catholic youth of Hanoi which, in the Government troops, furnished all by itself the effectives of several 'assault battalions.' (89)

For a while, the Catholics enjoyed a preferred status within the Republic. The government did not intervene with the administration of the quasi-feudal bishoprics of Phat-Diem and Bui-Chu and also treated the French and Spanish bishops with great consideration. A Catholic, Vu Dinh Tung, became Minister of Veterans Affairs (which he still is, as far as is known), and little or no interference was felt by the missionaries and nuns who were still free to go about their ecclesiastical duties.

On the basis of the evidence available it is hard to say whether the change in the D.R.V.N.'s attitude towards the Catholic Church was a result of the world-wide hardening of the Catholic Church's attitude towards Communism, or whether it changed in accordance with the general hardening of attitude of the People's Democracies against their various Catholic authorities. Nonetheless, and in spite of assurances to the contrary, from 1950 on, relations between the Catholic Church and the Government of the Democratic Republic have steadily deteriorated. The Vietnamese bishops, however, still maintained an attitude of strict neutrality, in spite of repeated overtures on the part of both the French and the Vietnam Nationalist authorities (90).

Suddenly, in the fall of 1951, the Viet-Minh took the initiative by attacking the bishopric of Phat-Diem by military force. French paratroops and ground forces saved the bishop in the nick of time from being captured, and war began now in earnest between the Viet-Minh and the Catholics, now ranged in their majority on the side of the Franco-Nationalists. Soon thereafter, the Republican Government initiated what appears to be a policy of expelling the non-Vietnamese clergy from the territory under its control. Thus, four European nuns and fourteen missionaries — including the 84-year old Rev. Padre Cadiere, known for his archeological studies — were expelled from the monastery of Viny, soon to be followed by the majority of the remaining minor clergy. Mgr. de Coonan, the Apostolical Vicar of Thanh-Hoa, is at present the highest-ranking Catholic cleric still residing in the territory of the Republic. Generally, the liquidation of the Catholic Church in the D.R.V.N. follows the pattern so well known from the People's Democracies: arrests of priests and the faithful, confiscation of church property, interdiction of correspondence with church authorities located outside the territory of the Republic, excessive taxation of church lands and buildings, etc. (91)

On the other hand, the Democratic Government has not entirely abandoned the use of propaganda designed to attract members of various religious denominations. A "National Congress of Religions" was held during the first week of August, 1953 "...in order to study the religious policy of the Government and of the Lien-Viet Front." At the conclusion of the Congress, its members issued the following appeal

> ...The camp of democracy and of the world peace forces under the direction of the U.S.S.R. becomes stronger every day while the camp of the invading and warmongering imperialists...grows constantly weaker...
>
> The Government and the /Lien-Viet/ Front never cease to manifest their solicitude towards us. Freedom of religion is inscribed in our Constitution and expressly recognized by the statutes of the National Front.
>
> Under the enlightened leadership of our President Ho...we are resolved /to / conquer our independence, national unity and freedom of worship... (92)

This appeal was signed by the priests and bonzes, combatants and heroes of emulation "...representing the various Catholic, Buddhist, Protestant and Cao-Daist religions..." and purported to represent both the Republican and Franco-Nationalist zone. Catholic organizations have not entirely disappeared from Republican territory. As a matter of fact, they have been taken over by the Lien-Viet. The two major such organizations are the Hoi Cong Giao Khang Chien (Association of Resistant Catholics) and the Hoi Cong Giao Cu'u Quoc (Association of Catholics for National Salvation). Both organizations publish several newspapers and periodicals.

As regards the Catholics in the areas held by the Vietnam National Government, the Viet-Minh appears to have decided on a military solution of the problem. This seems particularly true in certain areas behind the main line of resistance of the French Union Forces where the Viet-Minh hold important guerilla bases. Thai Binh Province in the Red River Delta was twice singled out for particularly violent massacres of Catholic villages. At Cao-Mai, 180 Catholics, women, men and children, were reportedly burned to death in the village church after the adjoining French post had refused to surrender (93).

More recently, the massacre of 1,400 Catholic villagers at Than Thuong, also in the Spanish-Catholic bishopric of Thai-Binh, was announced in the world press (94); while in the autumn of 1953, People's Troops successfully attacked Bui-Chu bishopric, where they massacred four nuns and captured an entire boys' school.

The above reports seem to confirm the fact that the D.R.V.N., like the other Popular Democracies, has made its decision that it cannot fully rely upon the Catholic element in the population, and therefore seeks to achieve by force and intimidation what it has failed to obtain by propaganda and persuasion. This is regretable for the Republic since the Catholics represent the most active and on the average the best-educated segment of the population. Thus, in this field, as in most others, the Democratic Republic and the Workers' Party have acted true to the form of government so aptly described by D.R.V.N. Vice-President Pham Van Dong in the following words:

> Why is this power called...Democratic Popular Dictatorship? The dictatorship is directed against the imperialist aggressors...to vanquish /them/ is the aim and duty of the popular democratic power... that is why it is just and logical to qualify it as a dictatorship... (95)

THE VIET-NAM ĐANG LAO-ĐONG

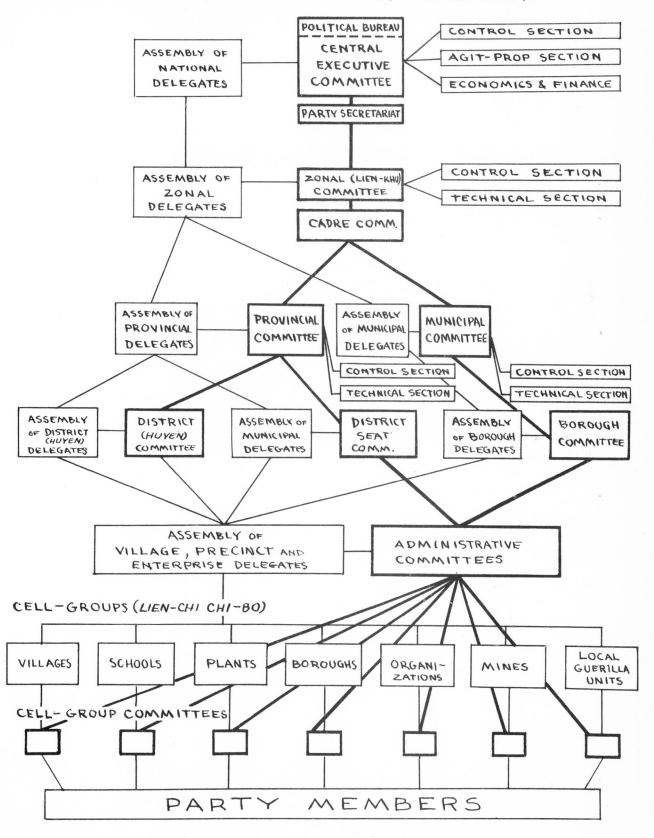

ORGANIZATION OF THE VIETNAM PEOPLE'S ARMY

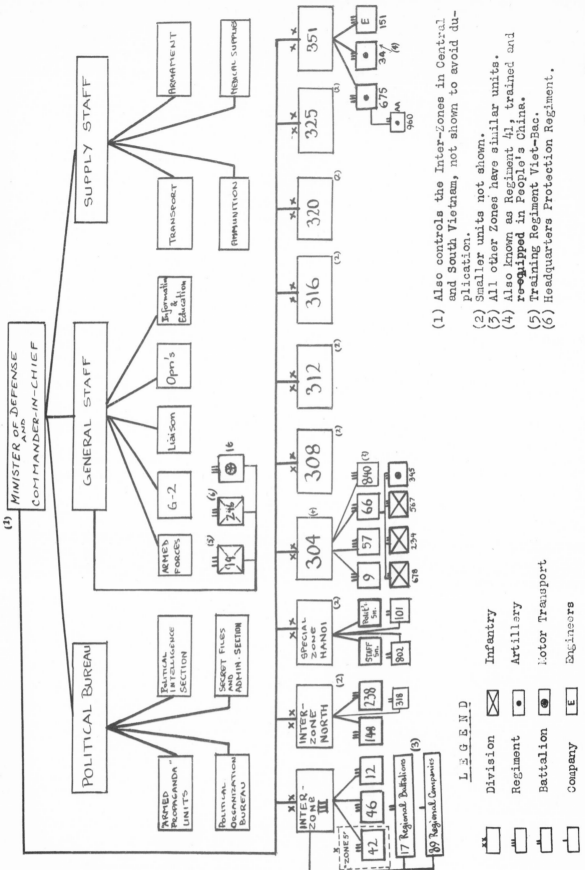

(1) Also controls the Inter-Zones in Central and South Vietnam, not shown to avoid duplication.
(2) Smaller units not shown.
(3) All other Zones have similar units.
(4) Also known as Regiment 41, trained and re-equipped in People's China.
(5) Training Regiment Viet-Bac.
(6) Headquarters Protection Regiment.

BERNARD B. FALL 3/22

FOOTNOTES

1. Cu'u Quoc, Viet-Minh daily, Hanoi, May 30, 1946.

2. Regards, French Communist Party weekly, No. 357, 1953, p. 21.

3. D.R.V.N., Radio Voice of Vietnam, March 19, 1953.

4. Id., March 13, 1951.

5. Pravda, daily newspaper, Moscow, 17 October 1928.

6. Zhukov, Ye, "The Crisis of the Colonial System," in Bolshevik, December 15, 1947, as quoted in Political Alignments of Vietnamese Nationalists, Department of State OIR Report No. 3708, Washington, 1949, p. 92. The fact is that it was French Communist cabinet members who failed to oppose the first credits for the Indochina war and French anti-Communist legislators never fail to mention the fact during parliamentary showdowns on the problem. The Communist reply is somewhat less than fully convincing.

7. "The Ho Chi Minh Government and Communism," in L'Union Francaise (daily), Saigon, December 29, 1948.

8. Dinh, "We are sure of Final Fictory," in For Lasting Peace, For People's Democracy (weekly), Bucarest, Rumania, 21 August, 1953.

9. Captured Document (unpublished), DLD Executive Committee Nam-Bo.

10. Captured Document, Circular 463/TV, Regiment "Cu'u Long," Central Executive Committee of Regimental DLD Cell, June 30, 1951.

11. Vietnam Dang Lao Dong, Statutes, D.R.V.N. Central Information Service, 1952, p. 1.

12. For a full copy of the Statutes of the CCP, see Brandt, C., Schwartz, B. and Fairbank, J. K., A Documentary History of Chinese Communism, Harvard University Press, 1952, pp. 422-439.

13. V.N.D.L.D., op. cit., Article 2(e).

14. Meisel, J. and Kozera, E., op. cit., p. 327.

15. Brandt, et al, op. cit., p. 423.

16. V.N.D.L.D., op. cit., p. 2.

17. Captured Document, Southwestern Cambodia, 1952, 6 pp., p. 2.

18. D.R.V.N., News Service, 1951, pp. 3-4.

19. Decree 149/SL of May 20, 1953.

20. D.R.V.N., Vietnam Information (Weekly Bulletin), Rangoon, Burma, No. 52/53 of December 31, 1953, p. 3.

21. D.R.V.N., Official Journal, op. cit., Decree No. 71, March 22, 1946.

22. D.R.V.N., Radio Voice of Vietnam, July 27, 1952.

23. Ibid.

24. D.R.V.N., Radio Voice of Bac-Bo, October 1, 1953, quoting Cu'u Quoc, Edition of Lien-khu III.

25. Ibid., Broadcast of September 17, 1953.

26. This error was often compounded by the fact that re-occupied villages saw the landowners come back with the French and Vietnam National forces. A recent decree of the Nationalist Governor of North Vietnam partially remedies the situation by "freezing" lands as distributed by the Viet-Minh before its departure.

27. D.R.V.N., Bac-Bo Morse Report, 14 September, 1953.

28. Ibid., 14 September, 1953.

29. Tin-Tuc (daily newspaper), North Vietnam, June 20, 1952. The writer has a copy of this issue in his possession.

30. Other illegal radio stations operating in Indochina are the Voice of Cambodia Issarak in Khmer; and the Voice of the National Resistance, both anti-Bao Dai and anti-Viet-Minh, of Trin Minh The, a Cao-Dai dissident.

31. D.R.V.N., Burma Agency (Morse code), 14 September, 1953.

32. The recent desertions mentioned in newspaper dispatches were exactly such desertions from among the troops of the feudal warlords of South Vietnam, unwilling to submit to the National Government, but nonetheless anti-Viet-Minh.

33. Captured Document, Report of April 22, 1953, by Hoi-Tuong-Te Cell No. 17 re the election results in Kian-An Province.

34. According to a survey made by the writer in North Vietnam, 82% of all civilians and military personnel deserting from the Viet-Minh zone could read and write. 2% had college degress.

35. Guéhenno, Jean, Education Populaire et Crise de Civilisation, UNESCO, Paris, 1950.

36. See Part IV below.

37. D.R.V.N., Press Information Service, Nam-Bo, Broadcast of February 10, 1954.

38. The text refers to the World Youth Festival held in East Berlin in the summer of 1953.

39. Title of affectionate reverence given Ho Chi Minh.

40. It is remarkable that a Communist speaker would refer to the mythical origin of the Vietnamese, as descendants of a goddess and a dragon.

41. Cf. the famous Henry Martin affair of 1951, in which a French Navy petty officer was found distributing such leaflets aboard French naval units.

42. Courtade, Pierre, op. cit., p. 35.

43. Halle, Guenther, Légion Etrangère (in German), Ed. Volk und Welt, Berlin 1952, p. 219.

44. Ibid., the book, based upon case histories of former German Foreign Legionnaires, even gives the names of the Soviet pilots, the Soviet plane identification numbers, and the itinerary flown by the repatriated prisoners from China to East Germany; pp. 273-276. The book is printed in the Soviet zone of Germany.

45. New York Times, January 5, 1954.

46. D.R.V.N., Information Bulletin, Rangoon, op. cit., No. 1/54 of January 7, 1954, p. 4. Italics mine.

47. Le Monde, Paris, January 16, 1954. See also the recent book by a repatriated French paratrooper, Goëldhieux, Claude, Quinze mois chez les Viets, Julliard Ed., Paris, 1953.

48. Ibid., No. 3/54 of January 21, 1954, broadcase by pilot-sergeant Guidoni.

49. Regards, op. cit., p. 9.

50. According to direct information obtained by the writer, the D.R.V.N. for a time considered obtaining from the French a promise of neutralization from war action and aerial bombing of a certain town in North Vietnam to be used as a safe haven for the diplomatic mission accredited to the Viet-Minh government. The project never materialized.

51. The Chinese World, San Francisco, April 12, 1954.

52. Abbreviation for "Liberation Party of Vietnam, Laos, Cambodia, Burma and Thailand for the Salvation of the Fatherland."

53. Classified French source. Similar sources indicate that there are certain fully identified Vietnam People's Army units stationed in Burma, for the protection of the Co-Ordination Committee.

54. See also Singapore Standard (daily), Singapore, January 4, 1953.

55. The problem is further complicated in the case of Vietnamese holding French citizenship. Under present legislation, they cannot even be deported back to Vietnam!

56. The Rapport Revers was a top-secret survey made by the then French Chief of Staff of the situation, the needs and the military aims of the French Expeditionary Corps. The resulting scandal of its leaking out led to the dismissal of Generals Revers and Mast, to a political crisis in France, and eventually to major military disasters on the China-Tonkin border late in 1950.

57. Le Monde, March 13, 1954. The Monde's title, stating that the conversations took place in 1952, appears to be in error. In fact, the article then goes on to state that the conversations took place "before the Laos offensive" (April 1953) and another official source (see footnote 60 below) also cites 1953 as the correct date.

58. Ibid.

59. Mr. Paul Mus, a French professor and expert on Indochina affairs, was sent on a peacemaking mission to Ho Chi Minh in the spring of 1947. French conditions -- which included disarmament of the Viet-Minh forces and unconditional surrender of men who had deserted to the Viet-Minh -- were judged unacceptable by Ho Chi Minh and the talks failed.

60. Office of the Vietnamese High Commissioner in France, Viet Nam (bi-weekly bulletin), No. 72, April 1, 1954, p. 16.

61. Le Monde, op. cit.

62. Vietnam has about 24-1/2 million people; while Cambodia has less than 4 million and Laos less than 2 million. Vietnam has a birthrate that doubles its population every 37 years, while the birthrate of the two latter countries is almost stationary.

63. See full quote on page 35.

64. Christian, Pierre, Son Ngoc Thanh, in "Indochine," op. cit., No. 11/52, p. 49.

65. A temporary regional delegation of the Republican Government, having jurisdiction over Cambodia, South Vietnam and Lien-Khu V (South Central Vietnam).

66. Abbreviated from now on as R.C.P.P.

67. Captured Document, dated August 5, 1951.

68. Paragraph 2, Preamble of the Statutes of the R.C.P.P.

69. Radio Voice of Bac Bo, March 26, 1954.

70. Ibid.

71. G. William Skinner, Report on the Chinese in Southeast Asia, Cornell University Southeast Asia Program, Ithaca, N.Y., 1951, p. 23, estimates the 1950 Chinese population of Vietnam as about 750,000, with a proportionately small number of 75,000 Sino-Vietnamese. Mme. Henri Fortunel, Les Chinois et leurs activités économiques en Indochine, unpublished mss. completed in 1950 and quoted in Roger Levy, Regards sur l'Asie, Colin, Paris, 1952, p. 168, estimates that in 1949 there were 880,000 Chinese in Vietnam. These figures seem to be underestimates.

72. As a high French official pointed out in Hanoi: "After having suffered the indignity of foreign concessions in their own land, the Chinese turned the tables on us and forced us to sign an agreement that amounted to nothing less than the establishment of Chinese enclaves in Indochina."

73. This statement is limited to the local Chinese. For outside Chinese aid, see Part V.

74. D.R.V.N., Vietnam Information, op. cit., No. 445/VNS/R of June 12, 1952, pp. 7-8.

75. Radio Broadcast (Morse), No. 15/394 of September 13, 1953.

76. D.R.V.N., Vietnam Information, op. cit., No. 3/54, January 21, 1954, pp. 5-6.

77. The Chinese World (anti-KMT but pro-West daily), No. 63/32, San Francisco, February 11, 1954, p. 2.

78. The Thai chiefs have never fully recognized Vietnamese suzerainty over the territory and poor communications never made either a Chinese or a Vietnamese military campaign worthwhile. Thai Territory (not to be confused with Thailand) takes in the whole northwestern third of North Vietnam, between the Red River and the Lao border.

79. Referring to the Red River Delta, a Vietnamese ethnic stronghold.

80. Captured Document, Z.A.N.O., May 1953, p. 1.

81. This exceedingly clever move is in contrast with the minorities policy practised by the Vietnam National Government, which placed the administration of those territories under a Vietnamese minister and two Frenchmen, Mr. Ecarlat and Colonel Didelot.

82. North Vietnam Information Agency (Morse), 21 September, 1953.

83. The G.C.M.A. (Groupe Commando Mixte Authochtone) are, as their name implies, commando units mostly composed of locally-raised guerillas with a few French officers and N.C.O.'s, operating on a hit-and-run basis behind enemy lines. Beating the enemy at his own game, they are generally considered as successful.

84. Hsin Hua News Agency (People's China) Report, monitored in Paris on July 29, 1953; and Radio Peking, monitored in San Francisco, same date.

85. Le Monde (French daily newspaper), December 13, 1953.

86. There is a curious tug-of-war among the Catholic church authorities in Indochina, between the Vietnamese clergy and its four bishops; the French clergy and the Spanish clergy and bishops who are very influential in Vietnam. The Vietnamese clergy faces the dilemma of political vs. church loyalty, a dilemma which is shared by the French clergy in Indochina to a certain extent; while the Spanish clergy faces the dilemma between its loyalty to the Church and its strong dislike for the French in general. These factors must be borne in mind during the reading of the following pages.

87. Renaud, Jean, Ho-Chi-Minh, Abd-el-Krim et Cie, Ed. Boussac, Paris, 1949, p. 235.

88. Bulletin des Missions, Vol. XX, Abbey of Saint-André-lez-Bruges, "Un appel des évêques vietnamiens en faveur de l'indépendence de leur pays," 1946, pp. 38-40.

89. Ibid., "L'Emancipation du Sud-Est Asiatique. 2. Le Viet-Nam," Vol. XXII, pp. 60-81.

90. Their neutralism then was absolute. Mgr. Ubernia, the Spanish Bishop of Thai-Binh, even relieved one of his priests who on his own had organized an anti-Viet-Minh village militia.

91. Climats (French weekly magazine on colonial affairs), August 5, 1953.

92. D.R.V.N., North Vietnam Information Agency (Morse), September 10, 1953.

93. Journal Francais d'Extrême-Orient (daily), Saigon, September 26, 1953.

94. New York Times, February 18, 1954. A subsequent A.P. dispatch, however, reduced the number of known dead to 20 and reports 837 missing.

95. Captured Document, Address to the cadres of Inter-zone IV, December, 1950, pp. 10-12.

PART FOUR: FIGHTING A TOTAL WAR

1. Organization of the Vietnam People's Army.

The Vietnam People's Army is the final product of the original bands of
Vietnamese guerillas who entered Dinh Ca valley in North Vietnam late in 1944,
under the command of a young communist professor of history, Vo Nguyen Giap.
Organized on an official basis in 1946 (1), the Army of the Democratic Republic
is, in the words of its leader, Giap, first and foremost a political army:

> The military force is the Party's essential arm for any political
> aim. (2)

While there is no point in reviewing the ever-changing military situation,
it might be useful to note briefly the organizational structure of the
People's Army (see Chart III). Its overall strength is estimated at approximately 400,000 men, of which about 80,000 are grouped into seven divisions
(Dai-Doan), one of which is a "heavy" (i.e., artillery and engineering troops)
division (Dai-Doan Cong Phao). There are also a certain number of organically
independent regular regiments (Trung-Doan) and battalion combat teams (Tieu-
Doan Doc-Lap). Together, the above units constitute the People's Army's
masse de manoeuvre, the hard core of its regular army, or as it is called,
Chu-luc, the Main Force.

It is the Main Force which carried out the offensives which in 1950
broke the French fortified line along the Chinese border from Cao Bang to
Lang Son; which captured the Thai country in 1952; and which invaded Laos in
1953 and 1954. By now, those units have a firepower equal if not superior to
a normal Western infantry division, in view of their extremely low logistical
overhead. In fact, their armament in medium (81 MM) and heavy (120 - 122 MM)
mortars is superior to that usually found in Western units of comparable
size. The number of modern recoilless guns per battalion is thus far superior
to that allocated to French Union forces. Some of the equipment is home-made
in local arsenals which have become progressively better-equipped, but most
of it comes from the Democratic People's Republic of Czechoslovakia and also
from Red Chinese arsenals (3); while the bulk of the automobile equipment is
either Russian or reconditioned American equipment from Korea. In fact, a
great deal of brand-new U.S. equipment has found its way from Korea to the
People's Army in Indochina, since apparently the Chinese People's Army has
unified its equipment upon Soviet standards, while the Vietnam People's Army
can rely partially upon U.S. parts captured from Franco-Nationalist forces
to repair and maintain its American matériel.

Not all regular units are necessarily stationed on territory held by
the Republic. For example, during 1953, a sizeable part of Division 320 was
stationed behind Franco-Nationalist lines in the Ninh-Binh area, while the
regular regiments 42, 46, 50, and elements of Regiment 12 were constantly
infiltrated in the Red River delta as "backbones" of the regional and militia
forces (see Map 2). Such regional and local semi-regular units (Tieu Doan Tap
Trung Tinh) are indeed second-line troops and have neither the equipment nor
the transport facilities for maneuvering. Their assignment is either to form
a screen for regular units, or to carry out local attacks. Such units are
also known to exist in the principal urban centers in Franco-Nationalist
territory, in which case they carry the name of Dia-hat Quan. In Hanoi, the
chief of the Interior Forces is Khuat Duy Thien, former head of the Office of

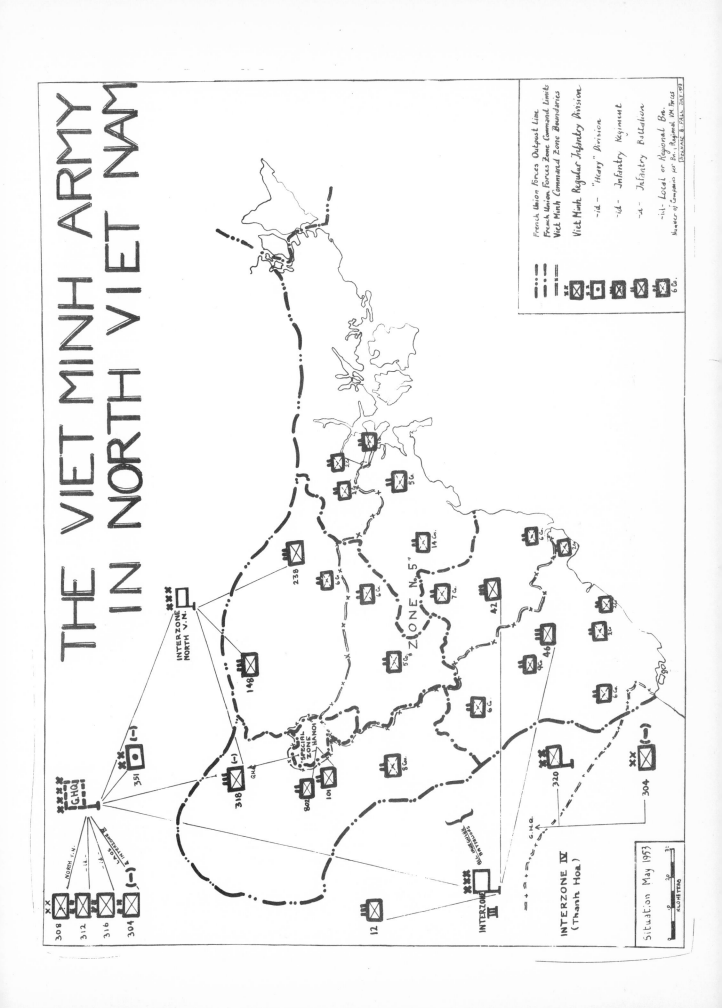

THE VIET MINH ARMY IN NORTH VIET NAM

Situation May 1953

KILOMETERS

INTERZONE IV
(Thanh Hoa)

INTERZONE III

INTERZONE NORTH V.N.

SPECIAL ZONE HANOI

ZONE No. 5

French Union Forces Outpost Line
French Union Forces Zone Command Limits
Viet Minh Command Zone Boundaries

Viet Minh Regular Infantry Division
–id– "Heavy" Division
–id– Infantry Regiment
–id– Infantry Battalion
–id– Local or Regional Bn.
Number of Companies per Bn.; Regional V.M. Forces

(BERNARD B. FALL JULY 1953)

People's Troops (regional forces) in the Political Division of the Republican Ministry of Defense. Two Chu-luc battalions (No. 802 and 101) are stationed within Hanoi, carrying out intelligence and sabotage work, waiting for the signal of a general uprising.

Lastly, the militia or guerilla (Du-kich) are locally-raised units, whose role is very important in the case of a Franco-Nationalist offensive. It is the Du-kich, unrecognizable because they wear no uniforms, who do the rear-guard fighting, sniping and reconnoitering, who hide emmissaries from the Republican-held territory, who bear the brunt of the "râtissages" (mopping-up operations). They may number anywhere between 200,000 to 350,000. They receive no pay, little armament, and carry on their farming or artisan work at the same time.

2. The Army and the Commissars.

The same decree which established the Republican Army also established its political watchdogs (4). Thus, even the lowest echelon (platoon) units have a "political agent" who caps the military leader. From battalion level upward, there are regular Political Commissars (Chinh Uy). At brigade or inter-zone (lien-khu) level, the commissar has at his disposal a special police and security detachment and a "Political Bureau" (Cong Cuc Chinh Tri), which, in turn, is subordinated to the Political Main Office of the General Staff (Tong Chinh Uy Bo Quoc Fong Tong Tu Lenh). The men of the political service belong to the Main Force and their uniforms are the same, with the exception of the background color of the rank insignia.

Their scope of power is extremely vast and their action is continuous and "...must make itself felt before, during and after combat" (5). They have their own newspapers and manuals, such as the Chinh Tri Vien Trong Quan Doi (Political Guide for the Armed Forces). In addition to the political services, there exist, of course, military security services which transcend all command channels and report directly to the inter-zone command (6). Thus, the tasks of the Chinh-Uy of the Democratic Republic greatly resemble those of the Military Commissar of the Soviet Army, whose instructions read in part:

> 2. A military commissar is a representative of the Party and the Government in the Red Army, who EQUALLY with the commander carries full responsibility for the fulfillment of all MILITARY tasks of the fighting unit... (7)

The Political Bureau of the Vietnam People's Army bettered at least the letter if not the spirit of the Soviet decree. A Presidential Decree of 1950, instituting "Front Command Committees with Political Preponderance," declares in effect

> Article 2. The Front Command Committee is composed of: a political commissar; a military commander; a deputy military commander.
> Article 3. In the case of divergence of views, the Political Commissar shall have the power of final decision. (8)

It was Vo Nguyen Giap's observation that the People's Army must be simply the military arm of "any objective" of the Workers' Party.

3. <u>The Human Factor</u>.

General mobilization of both men and women over 18 was decreed throughout the territory of the Republic on November 4, 1949. While there is no "draft" in the full sense of the word in view of the material limitations imposed upon the People's Army, recruitment begins locally and extends outward by stages. The recruit first joins the Du-kich of his own village. Then, if he is found physically well fit and politically reliable, he is assigned to a regional unit. Later on, if the situation permits and if the recruit again passes a more rigorous physical and political test (as well as a literacy examination), he is admitted into the "inner sanctum" of the Chu-luc, the Main Force. The latter thus receives "recruits" that not only have survived what sometimes amounts to years of combat, but also men that are a political as well as an educational elite. This partly explains why a high French officer once said that "Today, the Viet-Minh infantry may be rated as one of the best in the world."

The Chu-luc are comparatively well fed, with the basic daily rice ration set at 1.2 kilograms (about 3 lbs.). The rice is not only their wherewithal, but also constitutes their pay, part of which may be allotted to their families at home (9). The rice wages for officers increase up to 50 lbs. per day for a general. Thus, in an economy entirely based on rice, the Chu-luc truly constitute an economic elite as well.

At the other end of the economic spectrum are the "War Laborers," i.e., the men and women detailed to constitute the logistical support for the units of the Democratic Republic. If the lot of the A-frame carriers in Korea was a sorry one, they may take consolation in the fact that the lot of their brethren carrying 45-lb. loads in the steaming jungles of northern Indochina for fifteen to twenty miles a day -- plagued by climate, disease, wild animals, and the French Air Force -- is nothing but a never-ending martyrdom. Here again, the Communist sources themselves succeed in being more eloquent than any Western propagandist; the following is a collective citation for the Resistance Medal IIIrd Class for the porter group of Van Chan (Yen Bay province):

> ...fifty per cent of the workers of the war services of Van Chan are women...following step by step the People's Troops during the offensives, those workers had to climb many mountains and cross thick forests for months at a time. Often they covered 50 kilometers (31 miles) in one single night with heavy burdens on their shoulders.
>
> Each unit of war service workers had the mission of...(passage jammed)...five supply depots a day. The construction unit of Van Chan constructed twenty hangars in five days. Lacking tools, they had the initiative to use tree trunks slit into flat slivers as spades to dig into the ground...
>
> When it rained they covered the rice and ammunition which they transported with their own waterproof coats, in spite of the cold. Very often they collected the rice grains that had fallen along the way and added them to their ration...offering it to the troops. (10)

Or, as described by a French Communist writer in a recently published book much hailed by the Communist press for its "stark realism":

...a group of porters, among whom one noticed an old man with a white
beard and steel-mounted glasses on his nose; an old woman with a black
dress...the others were younger peasants and women. Some of them held
shovels in their hands and others carried baskets. Their clothes were
covered with dirt. They had taken refuge in the grotto after having
spent the night repairing a road which the /French/ bombers had cut
the day before... Thousands of men and women worked on those ravaged
sites, in the light of torches, among the uprooted trees... The workers
were grouped in crews generally from the same village. They defied
each other: 'Who is going to do better than the crew from Le Van Ba?'
One crew accepted the dare and they would work untiringly... Sometimes their work was interrupted by the explosion of bombs with
delayed fuses...the dead were taken away and work started anew... (11)

Similar acts of prowess are reported concerning mass mobilization into
the Armed Forces. In a report on the success of mass mobilization, the
Democratic Republic's Central Information Office pointed out on September 9,
1953:

...The enlistment of young men in the ranks of our Army was carried
out with great enthusiasm. Ten soldiers were to be recruited in the
village of Phuc Xuan, but 721 volunteers presented themselves. And
in Nha Long, thirty were required; forty-six volunteers were found... (12)

There is also widespread propaganda for the use of children in the war
effort, both as fighters and as laborers: the case is cited of the 12-year-old
"Child Hero," Hoang Huu Thu, who (according to Viet-Minh reports) blew up
the French intelligence bureau at Kien-An; or the children's group "Tran Quoc
Toan" which, in the summer of 1953, killed "three million mosquitoes and
19,000 rats"; or the school children of Nghe An province who dug irrigation
ditches; while the children of Duc Hiep (in Quang Nam Province) "...themselves
pulled the plows since there were no buffaloes..." (13)

4. Logistics.

It is chiefly with the help of such primitive means multiplied by a huge
number of individuals that the Viet-Minh actually succeeds in winning its
battles, which are first and foremost logistical victories. Commenting on
this fact, a magazine published by the French Information Services in Indochina states:

It may appear as surprising that with the few means at his disposal
Vo Nguyen Giap has accomplished a tour de force. Without cement-
mixers or bulldozers; without steamrollers and with hastily-trained
technicians...in spite of the systematic bombings of the /French/
air force, French land and maritime surveillance, the rebellion
continues and Chinese equipment arrives in the North; it follows on
the heels of the Viet-Minh divisions which sometimes penetrate deeply
into the lines of the adversary.

This efficiency is essentially imputable to the veritable mysticism
of 'the road at any price' which has been instilled in both the troops
and the population. (14)

We have seen in the preceding part how such strategic roads are being
kept open. It is, however, the hordes of porters who are attached to each

operational unit that constitute the logistical backbone of the Republican forces. Their use and existence conditions both the tactics of the Republican army and its present success. The long columns of porters are practically invisible from the air and invulnerable to almost anything except a direct ambush by French-led partisans or commandos-- a rare occurrence. They are also able to master practically any natural obstacle which they may encounter and are not greatly hampered by poor roads, blown-up bridges, lack of repair and maintenance, or any other calamities which may befall a mechanized transport service.

On the other hand, the "logistical overhead" (i.e., the ratio of non-combatants to combatants within the overall war effort) is enormous and cannot be measured with the yardstick generally applied to such services. To take a simple example, the average portage load for a daily 15- to 20-mile haul is reckoned at 45 lbs. The average food ration of a porter amounts to between 2 and 2.2 lbs. of rice per day. Hence, on a 300-mile haul, involving 15 days march, a porter is likely to have to eat 75% of his own payload which is thus reduced to 12 lbs. A simple calculation shows that in order merely to feed a Viet-Minh division on a forced march for 15 days, the same division-- for 12,000 combatants-- would have to be trailed by about 50,000 porters! And this does not include re-provisioning in armament and ammunition. The writer has been told by a Viet-Minh quartermaster colonel captured after the Viet-Minh retreat from Laos in June, 1953, that in fact, the two Republican divisions operating in the area had an aggregate supply column of 95,000 porters. Similar figures are frequently cited by both friend and foe, and may even be considered as conservative. It is obvious that with stepped-up aid from abroad, the Republic's logistical and depot dispersal problem might increase even further. It is, by the way, the establishment of many smaller intermediary depots between the rear areas and the various fronts which keeps the whole system from breaking down. However, such depots are vulnerable to enemy incursions and the capture or destruction of such a depot may well mean the actual destruction-by-starvation of the unit whose supply line has been severed.

A. The Motor Transport Service.

There exists, however, a service of automobile transport which circulates mainly in the northern inter-zones and is primarily reserved for the strategic transport of Chinese equipment to the main resupply points of the Chu-luc units. This service, under Dinh Duc Thien, controls nine truck companies of 37 trucks each, grouped into three "relay bases": Viet-Bac (Inter-Zone North), North-West, and Middle Region (Tuyen-Quang, Thay-Nguyen area). Each relay has its own administrative, technical and traffic sections. The central office further has an escort section (an autonomous armed unit which details guards to the convoys and drivers) and, of course, a Political Office. Each truck company also has its own repair shop. While the total number of motor vehicles in the Republican area is uncertain (there are some dozen vehicles captured intact from the French and Nationalist troops, and also some antiquated charcoal-burning Japanese vehicles), the total number of operational vehicles is estimated at about 600, with U.S.-made General Motors trucks operating in the difficult mountain areas (Thuy-Kau, Cao-Bang to Bac-Kan) while the lighter-built Soviet-made Molotovas are operated mainly on the Middle Region runs. This figure may be considered as conservative in view of the recently stepped up Chinese aid (15).

The People's Army also makes use of limited coastal shipping, particularly in the Central Vietnam area, whose many bays and inlets provide adequate

protection against marauding French fighter-bombers and navy patrols. Prior
to the total blockade of the Transbassac (South Vietnam), most of the strategic
rice exports, to be sold on the black markets of Bangkok and Singapore for
hard currencies or weapons, were shipped by means of sea-going junks. Recent
French communiques mention the use of small boats for amphibious attacks by
Republican units. There is thus far no Republican air force, but according
to French sources, the Republican Army has cleared several old airfields for
use as drop zones for supplies to be parachuted by the Chinese People's Air
Force (16).

5. Outside Aid to the People's Army.

The Democratic Republic of Vietnam is at present recognized by the Soviet
Union and all People's Democracies, and therefore receives a certain amount
of military and economic aid from those nations. While it is not officially
verified, mention is made of a lend-lease agreement contracted by the
Democratic Republic of Vietnam with People's China during Ho Chi Minh's
visit to Peking in April, 1950 (17). The impact of the new Chinese equipment
was immediately felt during the disasters which struck the French posts strung
out along the Tonking-Chinese border when the Viet-Minh offensive began on
September 19, 1950. By then, 20,000 D.R.V.N. troops were considered as fully
equipped with heavy mortars, machine guns and anti-aircraft machine guns of
various calibers. The troops included 29 light and 6 to 8 "heavy battalions"
which had received artillery pieces. The latter units were soon concentrated
in the "Heavy Division 351" (18). By the end of 1950, a full 40 battalions,
including 10 heavy, were fully armed by the Chinese, while Chinese aid for
1951 was conservatively estimated by French intelligence as amounting to
18,000 rifles, 1,200 machine guns and BAR's, 150 to 200 heavy (81 MM and 122
MM) mortars as well as about fifty cannon, a good part of which were composed
of newly-captured U.S. recoilless guns. Chinese aid for 1952 was estimated
to be double the above, so that now about 140,000 men may be estimated as
fully equipped (19).

By now, Chinese shipments are estimated at approximately 3- to 5,000 tons
per month, which allows the Republican high command to maintain its Main Force
on the ready and to re-equip its guerilla forces with the weapons discarded by
the Chu-luc in favor of newer and better weapons. The accent of Chinese
help seems to be now engineering equipment and heavier weapons, as well as
perfected anti-aircraft artillery. Artillerymen of the People's Army are
being trained on the gunnery ranges of Tsin-Tsi and Long Chow (Kwangsi),
China. Very recently, Artillery Regiment 34 of the "Heavy Division 351"
has returned from China, completely re-equipped with 22 medium 105 MM
howitzers. According to recent reports, such artillery has been successfully
used in action around the Dien-Bien-Phu airhead.

While most of the equipment is still captured U.S. equipment from Korea,
certain articles are made in other countries: trucks in the U.S.S.R., bazookas
and recoilless guns in Czechoslovakia, and many small weapons are produced
after European models in Chinese arsenals. The former 53rd Arsenal in
Kunyang, Yunnan, has now been re-equipped to serve the needs of guerilla
groups in Burma and the People's Army of Vietnam (20). It at first specialized
in optical equipment and light Czech-type machine guns. Renamed "South-Western
Arsenal" by the Chinese People's Forces, the arsenal was greatly expanded and
entirely re-equipped with Soviet machine tools and now produces ten types of
light weapons.

Recent reports appear to show a somewhat stronger amount of direct Soviet help to the Democratic Republic. The Soviet Union apparently has promised a certain number of transport planes, while jet fighters, reported seen on many new airfields around the North Vietnam border, have thus far not intervened in aerial combat (21). Nationalist Chinese reports from Taipeh, while generally somewhat sanguine, emphasize that a mixed military mission of 100 members, drawn from the armed forces of the U.S.S.R. and her satellites, has arrived in Nanning, Kwangsi province, China, to be

> ...eventually shaped into a military advisory group to oversee the entire Southeastern Asia communist campaign... (22);

while a first shipment of 37 tanks, built or re-built in Manchurian arsenals was sent to Indochina for duty with the Vietnam People's Forces. That a serious build-up of foreign aid to Ho Chi Minh is in the offing may also be seen in the speeding-up of the construction of a new military road and railroad from Kunming to Cheli, a Chinese town on the upper Mekong River, 170 miles north of Luang Prabang. The new road would be practically beyond effective French fighter range and would permit a speedier resupplying of Vietnam People's Forces operating far from their North Vietnam bases (23). Later reports show by now an estimated 300 Soviet advisers with the Vietnam People's Forces, while the Chinese People's Forces in Indochina act only in a military advisory capacity (24). True enough, there are about 20- to 30,000 Chinese now fighting in the Vietnam People's Army, but they are doing so on an individual voluntary basis and not as separate units. Special units of Chinese medical personnel also are engaged in Vietnam.

Such is the state of military co-operation between the Vietnam People's Army and its neighbors or allies of the Soviet Bloc. The "...close military co-operation between the communist and Viet-Minh armies in order to eliminate the bandits from the Indochina border regions..." has been openly hailed by the Chinese Communist press (25). It appears now that the Chinese People's Army might avoid the political error it committed when it openly intervened in Korea; this would forestall an open intervention of Atlantic or United Nations powers on the side of the Franco-Nationalists. In any case, further stepped-up military aid to the Viet-Minh might considerably narrow the already small margin between Franco-Vietnamese and Viet-Minh firepower and maneuverability. This would leave the latter-- all material factors then being nearly equalized-- in a rather advantageous position to continue the struggle on a basis that led to the Korean stalemate. This was actually foreseen by Vo Nguyen Giap in a magistral staff study carried out with the Political Commissars of Regiment 98, Viet-Minh Infantry Division 316, after the French disasters of 1950:

> The enemy thus progressively turns towards the defensive. The Blitzkrieg turns into a 'long-term war.' In view of this fact, the enemy finds himself in the following dilemma: he must make the war last /so as to win it/ and at the same time cannot afford to do so. (26)

6. The Doctrine of the Vietnam People's Army.

We have seen in the preceding chapters how the armies of the Democratic Republic have risen from the erstwhile guerilla bands and how they acquired their cadres, training and equipment. Still, while all those factors certainly explain a good part of the successes which the Chu-luc and guerillas have won over their heavier-armed and more numerous adversaries, this would be unthinkable without one additional factor: a successful politico-military doctrine.

There can be no doubt as to the fact that the Army of the Democratic
Republic has succeeded in developing such a doctrine. It is interesting to
compare the situation in Vietnam to that which prevailed in China prior to
the collapse of the Kuomintang armies, as was done in a very thorough study
by the former Commanding General of the French Far Eastern Air Force, L. M.
Chassin (27):

> One profound lesson must be learned from the Chinese drama: even in
> this century of materialism and mechanization, it is still the spirit
> which prevails, it is morale that wins battles. Nevermind whether
> one has men and arms if the former do not want to use the latter! ...
> The reason for Mao's success is that he succeeded in instilling faith
> into the Chinese peasants, and this by making use of thousand-year old
> reflexes...in the constant and patient effort of a daily political
> education. In the day's work of the Red soldier, the Marxist political
> lesson played a part that was as important as the arms manual. Taken
> in hand by intelligent masters, the armed peasant rapidly became a
> fanatic, an apostle of the new religion.../and/ in a civil war it is
> almost always the side which knows how to obtain the allegiance of
> the population that will win.

There can be no doubt of the fact that General Chassin's own experience
in Indochina seriously influenced his writing, which merely enhances the
validity of his statements. That General Chassin's conclusions have not
remained idle theory as far as the D.R.V.N. is concerned is shown by the
directives of the October, 1951, congress of the Workers' Party "laid down
by President Ho Chi Minh and the Central Committee of our Party...":

> ...2 - To intensify our struggle in the enemy's rear;
> 3 - Ideological reformation of the Party;
> 4 - Ideological and technical reformation of the army;
> 5 - To readjust the work of mass organizations. (28)

That such ideological training of the People's Army is a serious matter
is shown by the emphasis on long sessions of self-criticism, some of which
are even broadcast over the radio network of the D.R.V.N. No better example
can be found than the following example of the autocritique of Nguyen Chi
Chanh, Army General Political Commissar, during a conference of the Workers'
Party cadres of army units stationed in Lien-khu V:

> ...once the minute of silence had passed, the comrade at the rostrum
> publicly proceeded with the examination of his conscience. With
> severe eyes, he turned towards the national flag, then took the
> audience as his witness and said: 'Conscious of my responsibility
> to taking into consideration the point of view of the masses in each
> of my acts, I wish to recognize publicly my faults against the people
> and the Party'...
>
> ...there were the harsh criticisms of comrade Nguyen Chanh,
> concerning our mentality which had remained reactionary without our
> knowing it. He spoke harshly like a surgeon conducting an anatomy
> lesson upon a dissected corpse: 'There, there is an illness that
> must be extirpated,' and many comrades, listening to him, did not
> believe their eyes. They repeated to themselves: 'Nguyen Chanh sees
> clearly. He is a mirror for us. If we look at ourselves in a mirror
> we see our deficiencies; the errors he points out to us are evident.' (29)

It is clear that such a type of indoctrination would be hard to match in any Western country (and it would be highly debatable whether such an indoctrination would be desirable) but it is an everyday occurrence in the People's Army. Obviously, such a propaganda system breeds a type of discipline which practically excludes initiative on the part of the individual, not because the individual does not value his life highly -- a usual Western misconception about Asians -- but because such a political training conditions him to "...make the sacrifice of his life for better tomorrows" (30). Examples of such iron discipline of the "kamikaze" type are thus found very often among D.R.V.N. combatants. Their "dynamiteros" (i.e., groups attacking French fortified positions or tanks with hand-thrown explosives) generally make the sacrifice of their lives to accomplish their mission; and similar acts, merely because they are an example of good discipline, are often pointed out by Republican sources:

> During the attack on the /French/ post of Vinh Trach, the comrade Dai-doi Truong /company commander/ gave an order to the comrade in charge of the automatic rifle to rise and to fire upon the blockhouse. The comrade rose immediately although he was to be sacrified before he could even fire a shot. (31)

7. The Final Phase.

Generally speaking, the high command of the Vietnam People's Army has consistently followed Mao Tse-tung's basic strategic principles as laid down in his now famous article "Our Mission in View of Present Circumstances" written in December, 1947, whose main points may be summed up as follows:

1. First, attack only divided and isolated portions of the enemy;

2. Aim primarily at destroying the enemy, not at the capture of cities;

3. Do not fight unprepared battles, nor fight battles without hope of success;

4. Make use of all materials and of the majority of the personnel captured from the enemy;

5. Spread the ideals and spirit of courageous fighting, a willingness to make sacrifices, to overcome fatigue and to undergo continuous fighting, and as far as possible, deprive the enemy of all breathing periods. (32)

From the Viet-Minh point of view, the war in Indochina was split into three major periods for which, mindful of the above-enunciated principles of Mao Tse-tung, the Viet-Minh had worked out its own strategic blueprint:

1. Yield any town or terrain you cannot hold safely.

2. Limit yourself to guerilla warfare as long as the enemy has numerical superiority and better weapons.

3. Organize regular units and pass over to the General Counter-Offensive only when you are sure of the final victory. (33)

The first phase ended in the spring of 1950, when the French expeditionary forces failed to smash completely the Republican position in North Vietnam and thus allowed the Vietnam People's Forces to regroup around their mountain stronghold. The second phase found its high tide mark during the disastrous

fall campaign of 1950, during which the French forces lost their string of
border posts from Laokay to Langson. It was then that Vo Nguyen Giap
committed what may be considered as his only major error to date: he thought
the French ripe to be pushed back into the sea and sent his green Chu-luc
troops into the open flatlands of the Red River delta, where they were, of
course, helpless against the modern flat-trajectory weapons of the French.
In Giap's own words,

> At the beginning of 1949, having studied the internal and international
> situation, we launched the mission of preparation for the General
> Counter-Offensive (Tong Tan-cong). The preparatory mission is in
> reality included in the second phase. However, in 1949 the situation
> looked propitious, and the preparatory mission for the General Counter-
> Offensive was set ahead of time with the view of a shortening of the
> second phase. (34)

Giap dearly paid for his mistake in the battles of Vinh-Yen, on the Day
River, and in the Dong-Trieu hills, when he pitted for the first time his inexperienced Chu-luc units in open terrain against the flat-trajectory weapons
and fast-moving mobile combat teams of Marshal De Lattre de Tassigny. They
were severely defeated, but the grim lesson was learned, and thus far the
Republican forces have returned to step 2 of Mao's war doctrine, with
conspicuous success. Still, the specter of the Tong-Tan-cong, the General
Counter-Offensive similar to the one which sent Generalissimo Chiang Kai-shek's
troops to Formosa, haunts the minds of tacticians on both sides.

> During the 1st and 2nd phase we gnawed away at the forces of the enemy;
> in the 3rd phase we must annihilate them...
>
> II - When shall we pass over to the General Counter-Offensive?
> In order to pass over to the G.C.O., the following conditions
> must be met:
>   a. Superiority of our forces over those of the enemy;
>   b. The international situation must be to our advantage;
>   c. The /local7 situation must evolve in our favor.
> The international situation must be in our favor and we shall benefit
> from foreign aid in order to pass over on the G.C.O. /but7 merely to
> count upon such help would be proof of subjectivism and light-minded-
> ness. On the other hand we cannot underestimate its importance...
> ...other factors may also play in our favor: /enemy7 difficulties
> in political, economic or financial matters; protest movements against
> the war in the /French7 army and among the people.
>
> III - When we shall have reached the Third Phase, we shall use the
> following tactical principles to fulfill our strategic missions:
>   a. Mobile war, as principal activity;
>   b. Guerilla war, as a secondary activity;
>   c. Positional warfare, also secondary.
>
> IV - The Counter-Offensive Phase:
> ...The Third Phase may last over an extended period, because we need
> time /but7 our possibilities in receiving aid from abroad are also
> quite extensive. (35)

The most recent operations of the Viet-Minh Army in Northern and Central
Laos show that Generalissimo Vo Nguyen Giap had not overstated the tactical
and strategic possibilities of his force. His troops have made the most of

their inherent qualities of cross-country maneuverability and knowledge of the terrain, both in the offensive and during the long retreat marches from Luang Prabang and Takhek. While there are desertions of individuals (including those of officers and political commissars), there is little evidence of mass discouragement or low morale in the well-equipped and well-fed Chu-luc divisions, despite the fact that the struggle has now lasted more than seven years.

The battle for Dien-Bien-Phu, the French-held airhead in North Vietnam, might, however, very well be the straw in the wind indicating that Giap again feels strong enough in well-trained regulars and Chinese-supplied firepower to resume implementation of Mao's "Third Step"-- the much awaited General Counter-Offensive destined to sweep the French Union and their allied Vietnam National Forces off the northern part of Indochina which contains the vital Tongking rice bowl and the extensive military installations of Hanoi and Haiphong.

From the organizational point of view, the Red infantry divisions, with their hordes of porters and their light, yet powerful, equipment, might very well prove to be the ideal fighting unit for the vast jungle belt between the Gulf of Bengal and the mountains of South China.

FOOTNOTES

1. D.R.V.N., Official Journal, Decrees 33 and 71 of March 22, 1946.

2. Vo Nguyen Giap, in daily newspaper Nhan Dan, No. 26 of 20 September, 1951, rebroadcast by Voice of Vietnam, October 1, 1951.

3. See Part V.

4. D.R.V.N., op. cit., Articles 3 to 16 of Decree No. 71. See also pp. 41-42.

5. Circular No. 264 CTH, of 27 January, 1947, Political Division, D.R.V.N. General Staff.

6. Circular No. 1630/VF, of 9 December, 1946, Colonel Commanding 5th V.M. Infantry Regiment at Haiduong (North Vietnam).

7. Meisel, J., and Kozera, E., op. cit., p. 368.

8. D.R.V.N., Decree No. 32/SL, March 4, 1950.

9. D.R.V.N., Decrees No. 14/SL, 81/SL and 91/SL of 31 January, 20 and 22 May, 1950.

10. Voice of North Vietnam, September 22, 1953.

11. Courtade, Pierre, La Rivière Noire, Ed. Francais Réunis, Paris, 1953, pp. 61-62.

12. The figures indicated will have to be taken with a solid grain of salt. If a village that is small enough to be allotted only ten draftees produces 721 able-bodied men, something must be amiss with the recruiting system. Also, if in general able-bodied men represent ten per cent of the population, this "village" must have been a city of 8,000 -- and thus far, there are no such cities openly under Viet-Minh control. The comparative enthusiasm for joining the Viet-Minh army is often explained by the fact that "at least one eats there"...while the hapless porters merely receive survival rations and often have to bring their own rice along.

13. Voice of North Vietnam, September 25, 1953.

14. Guiges, Claude, "Logistique Vietminh," Indochine-Sudest Asiatique, Saigon, March, 1953.

15. Guillain, Robert, "l'Aisle Chinoise au Viet-Minh," Le Monde, March 19, 1954.

16. French Embassy in the United States, Document No. 26, November 10, 1950, p. 2.

17. Ibid.

18. Ibid.

19. Despuech, Jacques, Le Trafic des Piastres, Deux Rives, Paris, 1953, p. 143.

20. Sheng, Lu, in China's Voice (Chinese-language magazine), Hong Kong, June 15, 1953.

21. The Chinese World (English and Chinese), daily newspaper, San Francisco, No. 30, February 9, 1954.

22. Ibid., No. 32, February 11, 1954.

23. Ibid., No. 33, February 12, 1954.

24. Ibid., No. 34, February 13, 1954.

25. Kwang Si Journal (Chinese), August 1953, as quoted in Le Monde, Paris, August 21, 1953.

26. Captured Document, 17 legal-size pages, mimeo., October, 1950, p. 5.

27. Chassin, Gen. L. M., La Conquête de la Chine par Mao-Tse-Tung, Ed. Payot, Paris, 1951, pp. 232-233.

28. Truong, Chinh (Secretary General of the DLD), The Democratic Republic of Viet-Nam is Seven Years Old (English), V.N. Central Information Service, 1952, p. 19. For the increased accent on political training, see Appendix III.

29. Voice of Vietnam, October 1, 1951.

30. Gen. Chassin, op. cit., p. 233.

31. Captured Document, Report, October 1951, by Committee of Current Affairs, Zone IX (Nam-Bo).

32. There were in fact ten principles, but the other five merely elaborate on the above.

33. Fall, Bernard B., "Indo-China: The Seven-Year Dilemma," Military Review, Command and General Staff College, Ft. Leavenworth, October, 1953.

34. Captured Document, Study of V. N. Giap before Commissars of 98th Infantry Regiment, in October, 1950, p. 8.

35. Ibid.

PART FIVE: ECONOMIC PROBLEMS

To the informed observer, it might well appear that the "real" revolution which the Democratic Republican Government brought to Vietnam lies in the field of economics. From a colonial economy -- interspersed with islands of the traditional rice economy -- the country under control of the Viet-Minh turned within five years into an autarcic war economy embodying the beginnings of the Marxist agricultural system. In fact, it is the war itself which directly contributed to the creation of a complete and complex system of economic problems such as are generally faced by fully independent nations, for the traditional small-village rice economy -- once deprived of its French economic superstructure -- proved unable to provide the wherewithal for a mobile mass army.

It is the change from the primary defensive phase of the war to the secondary stage of mobile warfare which forced the Ho Government finally to face its economic responsibilities. During this secondary stage -- which appears to be still in progress -- the D.R.V.N. faced the problem of continuously feeding an important group of mobile units -- which cannot live off the land like the local guerillas, who fight mostly within marching distance of their home village -- and an even more important body of "war workers" (the porters), as well as a great mass of unproductive bureaucrats. The establishment of compulsory labor service for the two sexes (1), while providing the government with a certain mobile labor reserve, merely increased the problem of creating state-wide food and consumer goods reserves, and hence, the need for a certain amount of processing industries. This turn of events also forced the Republican Government to depart from its erstwhile idyllic policy of non-personal taxation and compelled it to put into force a set of stringent regulations in order to save its young and entirely rice-based economy from total collapse.

It is this new policy and its application in the industrial, fiscal and agrarian field that will be described in the following pages.

1. General Situation of the Economy.

The outbreak of generalized hostilities in 1946 deprived the Democratic Republic of all its urban production centers, which housed the bulk of Vietnamese industry that had gone beyond the strictly artisan stage. Soon, however, certain small mines in the Upper Tongking regions were put back into operation, not so much for local consumption as for limited exports to China. The following major mining operations are at present in progress:

a. Coal: Phan-Me produces excellent coking coal, considered as the best after the coastal Quang-Yen deposits; it is taken out via the Song Cau river to which it is connected by an 8-mile narrow-gauge railroad pulled by draft animals and/or human labor. At the southern end of the delta (see Map 3) the coal beds of Phu Nho Quan and Chi-Ne are known to produce good quality steam coal. Total coal production is estimated at no more than 50,000 tons per year, however.

b. Metals: Tin, wolfram and uranium phosphates are found at Pia-Quac, while a 75 per cent pure iron ore is mined in open-air pits at Tinh-Tuc. Available figures (2) show a present annual production rate of 300 tons of pure tin and about 90 tons of tungsten, and unknown quantities of uranium

VIET-MINH ECONOMY in NORD VIET-NAM

Map labels (place names and provinces):

MON CAY, Dao Cai Ban, Quang Yen, Haiphong, Kien An, Dao Cat Ba, Do Son, CAO BANG, Cao Bang, Dong Khé, Khao Ky, Nha Phuc, BACKAN, BacKan, Cho Moi, LANG SON, Lang Son, BAC GIANG, Bac Giang, Bac Ninh, Gia Lam, Hai Duong, Vinh Yen, Hung Yen, Thai Binh, Bui Chu, THAI NGUYEN, Thai Nguyen, Cho Phong, Duyen Hung, Phat Diem, Tinh Tuc, Fe, Ha Gian, Fe, HA GIANG, Ha Giang, TUYEN QUANG, Tuyen Quang, Chiem Hoa, Vinh Yen, Phuc Yen, HANOI, HADONG, Ha Nam, Nam Dinh, Ninh Binh, Phu Tho, PHU THO, Hoa Binh, Nam Duc, HOA BINH, Yen Lao, Vinh Loc, Thanh Hoa, Fe, Nhu Xuan, Yen Bay, YEN BAY, Cha Pa, Lao Kay, LAO KAY, Lai Châu, LAI CHAU, Son La, SON LA

Compass: N, S

LEGEND

■	Supply depots for outside aid
△	Industrial areas
N	Power stations in operation
▦ (vertical lines)	Rice surplus areas in V.M. territory
▨	Coal mines known to be in operation
⬡	Metal mines known to be in operation
⬭	Salt production areas
+++	Narrow gauge RR's in operation
=	Normal gauge RR's in operation
↓	The "Trade Corridor"

ore. Zinc is mined at Cho-Dien, at an unknown rate, but prewar capacity of Cho-Dien was 40,000 tons of 50 per cent pure ore per annum.

In the southern industrial center at Thanh-Hoa, iron pyrites are mined and treated locally at Nhu-Xuan, while a chromium mine ten miles from Thanh-Hoa produces approximately 2,800 tons per year of 50 per cent pure chromium ore. The Nhu-Xuan foundries also process scrap metal originating from dismantled railroad equipment and from captured unserviceable war material.

c. Power: It is in fact the problem of electric power and energy fuels that is the most difficult for the young industry of the Democratic Republic. Whenever feasible, human or animal power is liberally used. Some of the smaller electric plants operate on an intermittent basis, such as Ta-Sa and Na-Gan near Tinh-Tuc, and the small Ban-Thi dam near Cho-Dien. There also exists a certain number of small generator-powered electric plants, such as those which formerly belonged to French forestry industries, but they are hampered by the lack of spare parts and the absence of adequate quantities of fuel. Two manioc stills near Tuyen-Quang and Phu-To produce appreciable amounts of industrial alcohols which are used as fuels for electric generators. People's China also furnishes a certain amount of both fuels and generators.

2. The War Industry.

It is clear that under the present circumstances, the Democratic Republic has little choice but to subordinate the development of its whole industry to the requirements of its war effort (3). According to French sources, "...the enemy industry has now reached the workshop stage...," a far cry from its artisan beginnings. Some of the workshops now employ up to 200 workers and produce a great array of weapons and ammunition.

The general characteristics of the Viet-Minh war industry are its dispersion and decentralization, so as to limit the losses in case of French air attacks. However, a certain reconcentration has been noticed of late, due to the fact that overdispersion is prohibitive in terms of transportation costs (4) and also in view of the increased protection against air raids by anti-aircraft guns. The industry works on a basis of two shifts of nine hours each. Each group of plants is protected by a "forbidden zone," and industrial workers are very limited in their freedom of movement. They cannot change jobs if they want to and must live within the plant compound with their families. The present industrial labor force is estimated at 25,000 workers.

A. Organization of the War Plant.

While there are some private artisan workshops that produce for the war effort, the overwhelming majority of the war plants is nationalized, or rather created and owned by the government (5). The whole armament industry is organized as follows: a central Direction of Armament Production (Ban Giam Doc), with four subordinated services for armament, administration, a political commissariat and a security service. This pattern is repeated down to lien-khu and plant level. At the latter level, there are two committees, the Enterprise Committee (Uy Ban Xi Nghiep) and the Specialists Committee (Uy Ban Chuyen Mon). The first embodies the administrative and political control of the plant, while the latter groups the technical personnel.

This superstructure, then, controls the various stages of production (explosives, chemicals, supply, etc.) through the presence of a delegate of each of the two committees in each of the various production stage "cells" (Nganh). Every Nganh, in turn is composed of a certain number of groups (Toan), each of which participates in one single stage of production.

B. Organization of Industry.

There exist now two major industrial complexes in the Viet-Minh-held zone: the "southern redoubt" around the Thanh-Hoa rice basin; and the "northern redoubt" in Middle and Upper Tongking. The former serves the needs of the Lien-khu III and IV and of the regular divisions 304, 320 and 325 and in its 40-odd workshops produces light mortars, bazookas, recoilless guns and assorted types of ammunition. While the southern zone enjoys a better overall location and is situated in the middle of a good communications network and of an abundant labor reservoir, it has to depend upon raw materials from the Viet-Bac to the north in order to insure its production. The only surplus materials which may be exported from the Than-Hoa industrial redoubt are iron pyrites and chromium.

The northern redoubt is the real heart of the industry of the Democratic Republic. Reorganized during the latter part of 1951 into geographically more concentrated units, its five major industrial zones have also been the main beneficiaries of extensive foreign equipment and also of foreign technicians. They also have at their disposal the motor transport pool of the Public Works Ministry and benefit from very short communication lines from the production sites to the armed forces "consumer" divisions of the Chu-luc.

Despite its tremendous efforts, the industry of the Republic is still but a fragile edifice, and would hardly be worth mentioning under normal circumstances. Still, it has succeeded in introducing into a colonial economy the first elements of a "heavy" processing industry. There can be no doubt that the very existence of such an industry will bring about substantial changes in the economic make-up of the country after the cessation of hostilities. In the meantime, the economy of the Democratic Republic has to rely heavily upon foreign imports and also upon organized smuggling of consumer goods and strategic goods from the zones under the control of the Vietnam National Government.

3. The Taxation System.

After the brief period of euphoria in 1945 and the total collapse of the finances of the Republic due to the Kuomintang occupation and the subsequent outbreak of hostilities, personal taxes were re-established at a later date -- and many of them at higher levels than ever before (6). The Viet-Minh was even compelled to return to the old French system of unequal taxation according to the fertility of the soil (7).

During a chaotic period the following taxes were collected: the "Agricultural Contribution to the National Budget"; "Agricultural Contribution to the Regional Treasury"; special real estate taxes; a public tax on paddy; "Contributions for Nightwatchmen"; "Contributions" for popular education, regional troops, communal treasuries, and for the reconstruction of roads (8). At present the following taxes are collected on a regular basis:

a. The Agricultural Tax, which supersedes all above taxes, and which now is the mainstay of the D.R.V.N.'s taxation system;

b. Local Organization Tax, for the upkeep of the local administration, which should be deducted from the bulk agricultural tax, but which, most of the time, is added to the tax;

c. Real Estate Purchase Tax, based upon the purchase price;

d. Personal Income Tax, (1) based on net profits for industrial and commercial establishments; (2) based on gross income for small businesses and artisans; (3) based on net profit for capital gains;

e. Resistance Contribution, which is a per capita annual tax of 3,000 Ho-Chi-Minh piastres (9), and represents nothing else but the so-much-cried-about "head tax" of French colonial days;

f. Purchase taxes, on an ad valorem basis, and internal taxes upon circulating merchandise (10);

g. Slaughtering tax, of 10 per cent of the value of the net meat price;

h. Other taxes, such as a Market Access Tax, bridge and ferry tolls, special postal taxations, and business licensing fees whose increasingly steep rates tend increasingly to eliminate private business.

Other budgetary resources are Government Bonds which are pegged on the price or weight of rice, and thus are immune from inflation, which bring 3 per cent interest over a period of five years; Resistance Bonds which are placed at 100 kilograms of rice (or 30 Bank of Indochina piastres); and several other types of "voluntary" contributions (11), such as the "Winter Aid to the Combatants" and the "Tet (New Year) Contribution."

The list of individuals or organizations that are tax-exempted affords a significant insight into the workings and aims of the Democratic Republic.

The major tax-exempted individuals are the disabled war veterans, who receive a temporary tax relief for a two-year period; families with three of their members serving in the Vietnam People's Army; and finally the seriously ill and crippled. On the other hand, the personnel of the nationalized industries, of the central and regional administration, and of the local party cadres is permanently exempted from such taxes. It is obvious that such a measure, while truly affording relief to some of the citizens worthy of aid, in fact creates a tight system of political patronage which assures the government of the loyalty of its cadres, its army, and its industrial workers. It also shows that the bulk of the taxload has remained with the same group which has borne the brunt of taxation throughout the history of Asia: the nha-qué, the small rice farmer.

Indeed, the present taxload of the farmer in the Democratic Republic is worth some closer scrutiny, particularly in view of the recent legislation passed on the subject (12).

4. The Agrarian Taxation System.

The "Provisional Regulations of the Agricultural Tax" (Dieu Le Tam Thoi Thue Nong Nghiep) were promulgated as a decree on July 15, 1951 and were immediately hailed as showing great progress over the old taxation system of proportional taxation. The major innovation of the new taxation system consists in dividing the total crop of a farmer by the number of family members living off the proceeds of the particular farm, and by taxing the individual shares (13).

> The agricultural tax has as its basis the agricultural group, and is calculated according to the mean productivity of every individual belonging to the group...
>
> Every individual, drawing his livelihood from agriculture, counts as a 'part' in the agricultural tax, regardless of sex or age... (14)

In other words, the taxable "part" of the babe in arms and of the blind ancestor is equal to that of the fully productive adult farmer, this being accalimed as progress through "popular democracy" over the colonial system. It is interesting to follow the methods with which the Viet-Minh radio attempted to explain the new system to the citizenry:

> ...This system is simpler, both for the Government and for the people... Thus, last year, the farmer had to pay upon a crop of 8,000 kilos of paddy 6% upon the /first/ 2,000 kilos; 9% upon the /next/ 3,000 kilos; and 12% for /last/ 3,000 kilos. What complicated and long calculations had to be carried out! This year, the farmer who has collected 2,000 kilos shall divide the crop according to the number of family members... Thus, for a family of twelve members...
> 2,000 divided by 12: 166 kg 66; each one shall have to pay 12% of that figure, or:
> 16.66 x 0.12: 20 kilograms; and the whole family shall have to pay:
> 20 x 12: 240 kilograms. Hence, a great simplification for both the tax collector and the farmer. (15)

The bad faith of the above calculation is quite obvious, for, under the old system, a family with a revenue of 2,000 kilos per annum only paid 6 per cent, or 120 kilos of paddy per year. Therefore, the tax reform represents in this particular case a 100 per cent increase over the old rate. A further innovation was the elimination of a deductible tax-free basic income in the tax scale. Indeed, to follow the initial example of the radio commentator further points up the practically confiscatory tax rates of the new system.

Under the old system, 8,000 kilos of paddy would have paid a total of 750 kilos in taxes. Under the new system, even under the extreme circumstances of a 12-member family, the tax would amount to 2,240 kilos. In that case, the tax has increased from about 10% to more than 29% (16).

The last interesting element in this progressive taxation system is the table of tax brackets as published in the semi-official Cu'u Quoc (17). The nineteen lowest tax brackets apply to harvests which-- even untaxed-- would leave the farmer on the brink of starvation, while the highest tax bracket (45%) still leaves the rich farmer with twice as much as his minimum survival ration (18). Thus, the new form of agricultural taxation adversely affects the very small farmer -- and he is overwhelmingly in the majority in North Vietnam where 88% of the farms are smaller than 2.4 acres -- while it leaves untouched the industrial plantations and the large estates of the landowners. It was never intended to distribute such large estates to their tenants or users, but rather they were to become state property (19), to be worked upon by the same landless peasants as before.

Therefore, the new agricultural taxation system may be considered as an effective weapon to transfer to the state an important amount of the agricultural land without having to resort to collectivization measures which would be repugnant to the independent-minded Vietnamese farmer. The further implementation of the new agrarian reform, in combination with the measures outlined above, will bring about a progressive collectivization of the land within the boundaries of the Democratic Republic (20).

5. Fiscal and Customs Services.

As shown in the previous sections, the economy of the Democratic Republic is essentially based on the rice produced either within its own territory or the territory occupied by the Vietnam National Government. However, the Republic's outside purchases have to be settled in a more compact merchandise or in an internationally recognized currency. For the time being, the piastre of the Banque de l'Indochine ($ BIC) is such a currency, while the "$ HCM," first printed locally and then imported from Czechoslovakia, has not only failed to gain international recognition, but has been engaged in a dizzy inflationary spiral since the day of its inception. Its present approximate value is 1/6,000 of its "BIC" counterpart on the local market.

However, the D.R.V.N. has understood how to make fullest use of the high-value currency circulating in enemy territory so as to obtain various products which it can obtain only in the Franco-Nationalist zones or in Hong Kong or Thailand. It created three tightly-controlled "customs areas" throughout the whole territory of Vietnam (21):

a. the "free zone," i.e., the territory over which the D.R.V.N. exercises full and constant control, and in which the $ HCM is the only legal tender;

b. the "border zone," which is a belt of varying depth (8 to 15 miles) drawn around all Nationalist areas, in which both currencies circulate and in which transactions even with the Republican Government may be settled in $ BIC; finally,

c. the "occupied zone," which is the territory under Franco-Nationalist control, and which deals entirely in $ BIC.

A. Customs.

It is obvious that to enforce such a system requires stringent controls at the limits of the various zones, and the D.R.V.N. has set up such a network of regular customs stations which make interchanges between the territory occupied by the Republic and that held by the Franco-National forces equivalent to trade with a hostile foreign power. There exist four organizations in charge of the regulation, control and taxation of such trade (22):

a. the Committee of Import and Export Administration, which is subordinated to the Ministry of Finance and its zonal and provincial branches; and which, in turn, controls the

b. Office of Foreign Commerce, in charge of organizing the movement of "exports" from the Viet-Minh zone;

c. the Import-Export Service, which supervises the general flow of

VIET-MINH REVENUE SYSTEM

JULY 1953.

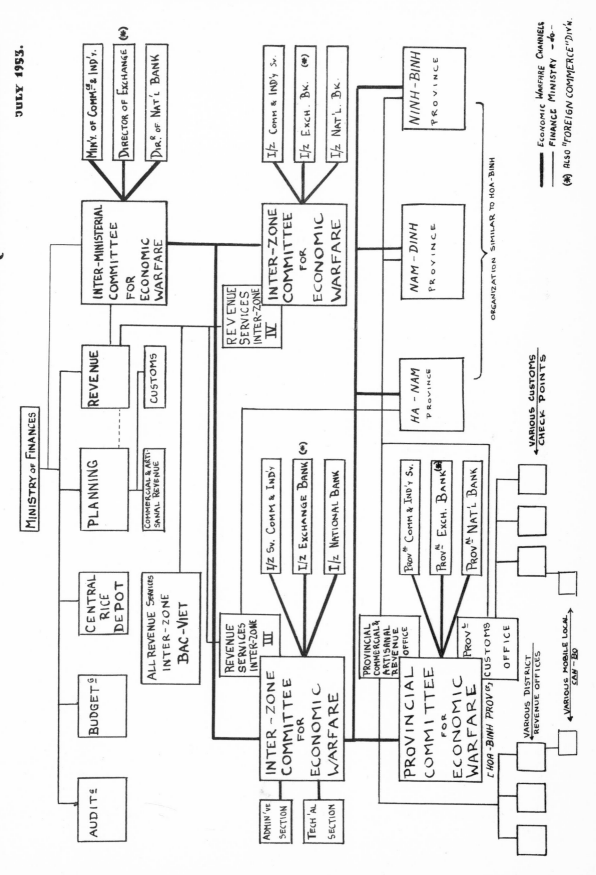

MINISTRY OF FINANCES

AUDIT⁰ · BUDGET⁰ · CENTRAL RICE DEPOT · PLANNING · REVENUE

INTER-MINISTERIAL COMMITTEE FOR ECONOMIC WARFARE

Minᵧ. of Commᶜᵉ & Indᵧ. · Director of Exchange (*) · Dirᴿ of Natʟ Bank

Commercial & Artisanal Revenue · Customs

All Revenue Services Inter-Zone BAC-VIET

Revenue Services Inter-Zone III

INTER-ZONE COMMITTEE FOR ECONOMIC WARFARE

Adminᵛᵉ Section · Techᴬʟ Section

I/z Sᵥ. Comm & Indᵧ · I/z Exchange Bank (*) · I/z National Bank

Provincial Commercial & Artisanal Revenue · Provˡ Customs Office

PROVINCIAL COMMITTEE FOR ECONOMIC WARFARE

[HOA-BINH PROVˢ]

Provˡ Commᵉ & Indᵧ Sᵥ · Provᴬˡ Exch. Bank(*) · Provᴬˡ Natʟ Bank

VARIOUS DISTRICT REVENUE OFFICES

VARIOUS MOBILE LOCAL CAN-BO

Revenue Services Inter-Zone IV

INTER-ZONE COMMITTEE FOR ECONOMIC WARFARE

I/z Comm & Indᵧ Sᵥ. · I/z Exch. Bk. (*) · I/z Natʟ. Bk.

HA-NAM Province · NAM-DINH Province · NINH-BINH Province

ORGANIZATION SIMILAR TO HOA-BINH

VARIOUS CUSTOMS CHECK POINTS

——— ECONOMIC WARFARE CHANNELS
————— FINANCE MINISTRY –o–
(*) ALSO "FOREIGN COMMERCE" DIVⁿ.

merchandise and controls the inflow of essential products by establishing
the various customs tariffs;

d. the Provincial Exchange Service, which is especially entrusted with
gathering the precious "foreign currencies" (i.e., the $ BIC, or occasional
U.S. dollars) brought in by merchants returning from non-Republican zones, and
with exchanging them into HCM piastres; and lastly,

e. the Auxiliary Collectors of Import-Export Taxes, who circulate mostly
in the "border zone" and collect the taxes upon in- or outgoing merchandise,
pursue defrauders, and, in general, perform the duties normally assigned customs
agents at the points of entry into a foreign country. All merchandise entering
the Republican zone must follow certain designated "trade lanes" (23), and
must at all times be accompanied by the customs receipt delivered by the
competent customs agent.

Such taxes are sometimes collected in advance deep inside the Franco-
National zone by roving cadres or can-bo who carry a regular receipt book
with them and circulate at night to collect their "taxes." Each of them has
several "helpers." They all hand in both the receipt stubs and funds to the
can-bo at huyen level and establish a cumulative report of receipts every ten
days. They have no power to remit or to modify taxes.

The tariffs are established by the central government itself and vary
greatly from one type of merchandise to another, according to its relative
priority in the war effort. Thus, there is a 100 per cent ad valorem tax on
bicycles (a "luxury"), while there is only a 10 per cent duty on medicinal
products, and no tax whatever on radio sets, explosives and machine tools,
which are vital to the war effort.

B. The Internal Revenue Services.

As shown in Part III, various taxes are collected from the population
throughout Vietnam; that is, the population of the Franco-Nationalist zone
in fact pays twice, once to the Vietnam Nationalist tax collector, and a
second time, at night, to the "finance" can-bo of the D.R.V.N., with dire
reprisals in case of non-compliance (24). The Viet-Minh collects taxes on
nearly every private vehicle and truck circulating in the Franco-Nationalist
zone, from 600 $ BIC for a small car to 5,000 $ BIC for a big truck (25), and
on every business, big or small, Vietnamese, Chinese or French. It has been
discovered that more often than not, it is one of the "substantial"
citizens-- one of the least suspected of collusion with the Viet-Minh-- who
acts as the local tax collector for the Viet-Minh, either willingly or under
threat.

The merchants and businessmen (in both zones) are grouped for taxation
purposes into merchants' "nests" of 15 to 20 who have to assess their own
earnings. This psychologically is a very sound move, for each one of the
merchants in the "nest" will see to it that his neighbor does not underassess
himself. If the total figure thus reached agrees with what the can-bo
estimates as a fair amount, there is no further question. If the desired
amount is not reached or a member of the "nest" does not agree to his share,
a second "nest" meeting is held. After a second failure to agree, the can-bo
steps in and his decision is final. If necessary, the can-bo may require
the assistance of the political section of the UBKC/HC.

The taxes collected by the Viet-Minh in the Vietnam National zones are
often quite heavy: in Nam-Dinh, for example, a 10% paddy tax is collected
on rice land, while a "head tax" of $ BIC 5.00 is paid to the Viet-Minh by
all residents of the Nationalist zone (26).

The Can-Bo

A word must be said about the unique personage that is the can-bo or
cadre representative of the regime. In the present case, the finance can-bo
is a man whose scrupulous honesty with the often very important amounts of
public funds that are entrusted to him has become proverbial throughout
Vietnam. Cases have been cited of can-bo who have been captured in states
of extreme malnutrition and exhaustion, carrying upon them amounts of money
which would certainly have insured their wealth, or in any case a comfortable
living. Even deserters from the Viet-Minh zones do not fail to pay homage to
the quasi-religious zeal of the can-bo of the D.R.V.N. revenue system:

> In view of the fact that the revenue can-bo are in close touch with
> the merchants, the latter do not resent them. The merchants have
> noticed that those agents only execute orders from above and that
> they lead a modest life. (27)

No greater homage could be asked for in a country -- or a continent --
where nepotism, graft and "squeeze" was an established century-old custom of
the revenue system. The finance can-bo also undergoes a rigorous training
for his job. He receives courses on the theory of revenue laws and decrees;
then is given "field training" by making statistical compilations of shopkeepers and others, and later on learns how to group merchants into "nests,"
and teaches the various "nests" elementary accounting methods. He must also
be able to explain the current tax legislation to the various shopkeepers of
his district (28).

C. Banking.

There exists two types of banks; the Import-Export Banks (Ngan-hang Xuat-
nhap Khau), which handle the exchange of $ BIC's into Viet-Minh currency; and
the normal banks (Ngan-hang Noi-dia) which act as simple deposit banks and
handle only HCM currency. The bulk of the transactions, however, is carried
on with the Franco-Nationalist zone. As recent investigations of the French
Parliament in the course of the "Piastre Scandal" have shown, nearly the
whole illegal money market in piastres carried on in Indochina, Hong Kong
or Singapore eventually profits the war effort of the Viet-Minh (29). Likewise, the reevaluation of the BIC piastre (at 70 per cent) on December 25,
1945 -- intended to prime the economic pump of Indochina -- first and foremost
profited the Ho Chi Minh Government, whose treasury of BIC piastres found
itself increased by as much; while certain experts affirm that a devaluation
of the piastre in 1947 to a level which would have made black-marketing un-
profitable might have very well caused the financial collapse of the Republican
Government (30).

Communist sources have made mention of a Republican gold currency, the
Dong Viet, which allegedly

> ...has a very high purchasing power. The Democratic Republic also
> emits gold pieces of 20 viets, a thing which the French Treasury has

not done for a long time. The French authorities are in fact forced
to recognize the Vietnamese banknotes and to accept their circulation.. (31)

Needless to say, no one has ever seen the Dong Viet, and to the best knowledge
of French Intelligence and of the experts of the Bank of Issue of Indochina,
the Dong Viet is at most a theoretical gold-standard monetary unit of undefined
value.

A currency reform carried out in the Republican zone on January 1, 1953,
swept away all the odd HCM piastres which had been printed by local and often
very rudimentary means, and replaced them by a new Czech-printed currency in
banknotes of 1, 2, 10, 20, 50, 100 and 500 piastres. The old currency was
exchanged at the rate of 100 of the old against one piastre of the new, which
wiped out the savings of the smallest holders but totally failed to stop the
inflationary spiral. The new piastre is now as poorly pegged as the old HCM
piastre.

Therefore, the Republican Government has more and more departed from
its policy of accepting paddy as a means of payment, and also has requested
advance payments of taxes in order to absorb at least a fraction of the huge
volume of currency in circulation. It admitted quite candidly in one of its
propaganda leaflets addressed to its own population:

> The expenditures of the Resistance require not only paddy but also
> money. Taxation in paddy forces the Government to resell the paddy
> to the population so as to receive money -- which would only be a
> bother and a loss of time... Especially in the enemy's rear area,
> the collection of taxes must be made in BIC money for two reasons:
> to face expenditures in the zones that need them; and to hurt
> severely the enemy's finances... The Government uses the money of
> the enemy and returns it to him to buy the merchandise necessary for
> the Resistance. (32)

That such measures fail to meet with popular enthusiasm is certain, but no
stringent war economy is ever generally very popular. However, the measures
taken by the Democratic Government have been so drastic that the Vice-
President of the Republican Government submitted himself to the following
auto-critique during a cadre meeting in December, 1950:

> ...Contribution Policy

> ...Our present policy shows the following abuses:

> 1) Mobilization of human resources: by mobilizing the population
> to the limit for resistance and military activities and not leaving
> it the time necessary for its agricultural activities. We thus
> hurt normal production while we talk about intensifying it.

> 2) By forcing the population to give rice lands, other lands,
> cattle and seeds, we take away part of its means of livelihood.
> By imposing increasingly heavy taxes above a certain level, we
> take away from the population the incentive to produce /more/.
> What should we say when we take away its means of work? (33)

The adverse publicity created by the application of such drastic reforms
in the field of taxation and agriculture compelled the D.R.V.N. to give firm
promises to the populations still in the "provisionally occupied zones"

...that the senseless requisitions which took place during the early period of Resistance, and which were contrary to the principles of democracy, shall not be renewed. (34)

The new agrarian reform law of 1953 might be taken as a test of the Republican Government's promise.

FOOTNOTES

1. D.R.V.N., Decree of September 1, 1952.

2. The information contained in this part of the chapter stems from sources close to the French Army which cannot, for obvious reasons, be identified.

3. For readings on the Viet-Minh war effort, the following articles in Indochine-Sudest-Asiatique, Saigon, will prove very informative: "Panoplie Vietminh" (July, 1952), "Logistique Vietminh" (March, 1953), both by Claude Guiges; and "Economie Vietminh" by André Clermont (June, 1953).

4. "Costs" of transportation have to be reckoned in terms of rice rations allocated for the human carriers, and constitute, therefore, a very serious factor.

5. Central Economic Section of the Central Executive Committee of the French Communist Party, Le Monde du Socialisme et de la Paix, Paris, 1953, pp. 163-165.

6. See Decrees 13/SL and 40/SL, D.R.V.N., 1951.

7. Nhan-Dan (Viet-Minh zone daily), No. 77, 9 October, 1952.

8. Decree 40/SL, op. cit., Article 1, para. 1, of July 15, 1951.

9. The Ho-Chi-Minh piastre ($ HCM) approximately equals $U.S. 0.000025. For example a bicycle worth $U.S. 30 is worth $ HCM 1,200,000.

10. D.R.V.N., Decree 44/SL of May 27, 1951.

11. The term "Contribution," less offensive than the French-used "Tax," has replaced the latter on most occasions.

12. See footnotes 6 to 8.

13. D.R.V.N., Decree No. 40/SL, op. cit., Article 2.

14. Ibid.

15. Radio Voice of Vietnam, May 17, 1951.

16. 8,000 : 12 = 666.66 kilos. Tax bracket for 666 kilos is 28%. 666.66 x 0.28 x 12 = 2,240.

17. Cu'u Quoc (daily), No. 2080, Edition of Lien-khu IV, of July 6, 1952, gives the full table of tax brackets.

18. Paddy, the unthreshed rice, loses 45% of its gross weight when treated for consumption. Thus, the following calculation must be made in order to arrive at the yearly minimum survival ration of the farmer: the daily average ration being calculated at 800 grams (less than 2 lbs.) of pure rice, it is multiplied by the "paddy factor" (155/100) and the number of days of the year: 0.8 kilo x 365 x Paddy Factor = 452 k/yr. Taxation bracket No. 1 begins at 71 kilograms per person. Thus even in terrain permitting two harvests a year, the farmer would be simply taxed into starvation -- or into abandoning his land to the State.

19. D.R.V.N., Article 8 of Decree No. 90/SL of May 22, 1950, which would thus tend to create a Vietnamese equivalent of the Russian Sovkhozi (state farms).

20. See Part VI on Land Reform.

21. For the information shown below, see André Clermont, L'Economie Viet-Minh, pp. 30-32.

22. See Chart IV on the organization of the D.R.V.N. Revenue System.

23. See Map 3.

24. Despuech, Jacques, op. cit., p. 125. His whole Chapter VII ("Finances and Economy of the Viet-Minh") is recommended reading on the subject.

25. Ibid.

26. Ibid.

27. French Ground Forces, North Vietnam (F.T.N.V.), G-2, Report No. -- of February 20, 1953.

28. Ibid.

29. Republique Française, Debats Parlementaires, Assemblée Nationale, July 2, 1953.

30. Despuech, op. cit., pp. 129-133.

31. Regards, op. cit., p. 14.

32. Captured Document, Spring, 1953, Office of the Commissioner of the French Republic in North Vietnam, Hanoi.

33. Captured Document, Address of Vice-President Pham Van Dong to the government cadres in Inter-zone IV, December, 1950. Captured during "Operation Lorraine," No. 6692, pp. 10-12.

34. Radio Voice of the Nam-Bo, June 17, 1950.

PART SIX: AGRARIAN REFORMS

The institution of agrarian reform, particularly in a nation where 90 per cent of the population lives by agriculture, is bound to have deep repercussions upon the development of the country at large. Such is the case in Vietnam, and both governments have attempted to solve the problem in their own way.

As in most other Asian countries, Vietnam's major problem is its enormous population pressure upon the relatively small fertile areas. In the Red River Delta, 9 million people live in an area of 5,790 square miles; in the Central Vietnamese deltas, 5.1 million people live on 5,400 square miles; in the Mekong Delta, 3.8 million people are concentrated on 6,180 square miles of fertile soil, while the recently reclaimed territories of the Trans-Bassac enjoy a relatively lower population density of 1.3 million people for 7,720 square miles of land (1).

The crux of the problem, however, lies in the apportionment of the available land. While in North Vietnam, 61 per cent of the holdings amounted to 1 mau (2) or less, in South Vietnam holdings over 125 acres take up 45 per cent of the available land (3). Collective ownership of land as a palliative to landlessness has been a century-old practice throughout Indochina.

> ...The community owns part of the land constituting its territory, the largest part consisting of land originally granted by the State to the village with the right to usufruct. People deprived of rice fields turn for support to the communal lands... (4);

the cultivation of which is re-apportioned periodically. Such communal lands represented-- in the 1930's-- about 20 per cent of the total arable area of North Vietnam; 25 per cent in Central Vietnam; and but 3 per cent in South Vietnam. Retrospectively, it might be said that one of France's most serious errors of policy has been to let the communal lands fall prey to speculators and to dishonest village chiefs, despite the warnings of experts of the importance of the maintenance or even increase of communal holdings, or at least the check of the increase of large latifundia.

This was not the case of North and Central Vietnam, where 98.7 and 90 per cent respectively of the total farm land area were tilled by owners (5), while South Vietnam's percentage amounted to only 64.5 per cent. Still, those percentages of owner-operated farms are "...larger than in many other Asiatic countries" (6).

Therefore, the problem of land reform (i.e., reapportioning of the land ownership) was acute only in the south, but not in the northern areas which are precisely those that are under the control of the Republican Government. The major immediate problem lay rather in the reduction of high and excessive land rents and other usurious practices, and the Republican Government has fully realized this. All its efforts in the first five years of its existence tended towards that objective. The implementation of the land reform was actually only begun when a satisfactory reduction of land rents had been obtained throughout the territory of the Republic. The subsequent enthusiasm for the Republican land reform was created more for its propaganda effects upon the Nationalist zone which, in fact, contains most of the big estates, than as a result of the reform's effectiveness in improving the status of the small farmer in the Republican zone.

1. Reduction in Land Rent.

The policy of reduction of land rent was carried out on an informal basis during the first years of the Republican regime, and the Lao-Dong Party Platform of February, 1951, again emphasizes that

> ...our agrarian policy at present aims mainly at carrying out the reduction of land rent and interest. (7)

This, at first appearance, very conservative program is candidly justified by the Workers' Party because the

> resistance has to be carried out in such a way that it can, on the one hand, bring a large number of landlords over to the cause of the resistance or at the very least neutralize them instead of pushing them into the arms of the imperialist aggressors...
> ...A big number of landlords have voluntarily contributed big sums to the resistance funds or donated hundreds of thousands of hectares of land to the Government. (8)

The following executive measures were taken by the Republican Government to implement its policy of mere rent reduction:

1. The Decree 78/SL of July 14, 1949, establishing the "Rent Reduction Council" and deciding a flat reduction of 25% of all rents (and 35% in certain hardship cases).

2. The Inter-Departmental Implementation Circular 152/NVI, of July 23, 1949, however, as in the case of the agrarian and income tax, exempts soldiers and government employees from applying rent reductions to their tenants, providing that the rented lands do not exceed 3 mau (2.7 acres) -- a move that could hardly have endeared the new ruling class to the populace.

3. The Inter-Departmental Circular 33/NVL, of August 21, 1949, published jointly by the Ministries of Justice, Finance, Interior and Agriculture, lays down the guiding principles of the distribution to the landless farmers of land belonging to French nationals or Viet-gian (traitors, i.e., pro-Bao Dai Vietnamese). The Circular stipulates, however, that all land grants were "temporary"; with priority given to disabled war veterans, families of soldiers killed in action, etc. It also creates the "Land Allotment Committees" in charge of the apportionment.

4. A Supplementary Circular of December 21, 1949, eliminates the term "temporary" from the above decree.

However, the free-for-all which resulted from the allotment of such lands was highly detrimental to increased production, for all less-productive or marginal lands were promptly abandoned by their tenants in favor of better located "abandoned" lands. This led to a new Decree on the Administration of Rice Fields and Lands (9) which reclassified all abandoned lands into three categories:

a. lands of collaborators;

b. lands of persons residing -- of their own will or not -- in "enemy" territory, but not actively collaborating;

c. lands of persons whose whereabouts are unknown.

In the first case, they are seized outright by the Government and considered as State property. In the second case, the Government may seize all or part of all lands of this category, each case being considered separately. They may also be returned to their former owners after deduction of all administrative expenses. In the last case, the State holds the property in escrow and returns all property to the rightful owner after deduction of expenses.

2. Abolition of Debts.

In another highly commendable move, the Republican Government attacked the second-biggest plague which besets the small Asian farmer: the usurious interest rates drawn from originally insignificant debts.

By Decree No. 89/FL of May 22, 1950, the Republican Government abolished all debts which had been contracted before 1945; and recent debts where the already-paid interest exceeded by 100 per cent the original principal, or which were contracted by individuals killed in action on behalf of the Republic. A last clause wiped out debts contracted against individuals convicted for "anti-state crimes."

Furthermore, a Production Credits Office was set up to provide the needy farmers with long-term low-interest loans, so as to make them independent of the still quite high interest rates (18% on cash and 20% on loans in kind) allowed private money lenders and landlords under the new legislation (10).

3. Measures to Increase Production.

However, all those measures -- while commendable per se and on the whole, very realistic -- did not contribute to the increase of agrarian production. Numerous landlords, knowing that they were about to lose part of, or all their holdings, failed to plant their fields or simply fled into the Nationalist zones, taking along their draft animals and farming implements, and many small farmers deserted their own plots in order to receive better lands without being immediately replaced by landless peasants.

Therefore, by a decree of the same date as the above, the Republican Government sought to alleviate the danger of a total breakdown of organized agricultural production by subordinating land reapportionment to the necessities of war, as provided for in the Decree No. 20/SL of February 12, 1950, "The total mobilization of all human, material and financial resources of the Fatherland."

The new Decree No. 90.FL of May 22, 1950 on Land Utilization and Apportionment contains the following interesting points:

Article 2 - All lands or rice fields which have been left uncultivated by their owners for a continuous period of five years after the date of promulgation of this Decree and which have not been subject to an intensification of production before the end of 1950, are declared property of the State.

Article 3 - All those uncultivated...lands will be temporarily alloted to poor peasants, after confiscation.

Article 4 provides for temporary apportionments of 10 years to poor farmers, with a tax exemption of three years, while Article 5 stipulates that in the case of lands left untended for less than five years the owner might be compelled to till them immediately or to have them cultivated by People's Troops, or to "...lend them to someone else for cultivation."

Should the owner refuse to lend his lands of his own free will, the local UBKC/HC shall intervene and regulate the conditions of the lease.

"In the case of intervention of the local UBKC/HC," states Article 6 of the same Decree,

the duration of the lease will be set at between 3 and 10 years, calculated in consideration of the state of the lands in question (easy or difficult exploitation, etc.). (11)

Finally, the same decree, which, retrospectively must be considered as one of the cornerstones of the D.R.V.N.'s agrarian policy, specifically prohibits the breaking-up of the large industrial plantations, against which the whole agitation for an agrarian reform had been directed in the first place:

Article 8 - The present Decree does not apply to:
1) Lands planted with industrial plants with yearly crops.
2) Lands left uncultivated because their owner, serving in the Resistance, is unable to cultivate them. (12)

Therefore, the Republican Government had effectively succeeded in killing two birds with one single stone: by taxing certain peasant groups practically out of business while at the same time forcing them to maintain all their available land under cultivation, the Government forced an increasing number of landowners to make outright gifts of their estates to the State:

Mr. Nguyen Duy Dien, landowner at Bac-Giang...has offered more than all his colleagues by giving the Government 700 mau /about 660 acres/ of rice fields and 19 buffaloes and additional cattle. Furthermore, in 1950 he has reduced land rents far below the figure determined by the Government... (13)

This policy was quite candidly explained by the quasi-official newspaper Nhan-Dan in an editorial on "The Spirit of the Present Agrarian Policy":

.../The policy/ aims at the confiscation of rice fields and other land from the imperialists, the Vietnamese traitors and reactionaries without, however, abolishing the forms of feudal exploitation or the system of ownership...of the feudal landowners. In the beginning, its only aim is to weaken the economic power of the feudal group and partially to satisfy the desires of the peasantry. In order to realize the present agrarian policy one must unleash the peasant masses so that they struggle against the landowners who form the social class that oppresses and robs them.

...It is, however, necessary to reassure the businessmen and industrialists so that they may develop their enterprises and

actively support the struggle of the peasants... The present policy
of the Party and Government consists in preserving the rich farmer...
They may still rent labor... If one borrows money from them one must
pay it back; if capital is involved, interest must be paid. (14)

This very recent article and other similar indications show that the
Democratic Republic, while using its agrarian policy as a medium of mass
appeal for the outside and particularly for the Nationalist zone, where the
agrarian problem is more acute, on its own territory practises a policy that
may well be compared to the New Economic Policy (NEP) of the Soviet Union in
the 'twenties. Still, it is of interest to see how much the above-mentioned
reforms and the "weakening" of the feudal and landlord class has profited
that perennial underdog: the small or the landless farmer.

4. The Small Farmer and the Reforms.

As has been shown on page 91, the average yearly survival rice ration of
a farmer may be set at 453 kilograms, or exactly 1,000 lbs. of paddy. In
Indochina, exactly one acre of rice land is required to grow an average of
1,006 lbs. of paddy (15). It is, therefore, easy to see whether the various
reapportionments of land carried out by the Viet-Minh have really succeeded
in alleviating the tragic land hunger of the Vietnamese peasant.

As a general rule, they have not. The figures quoted by sources of the
Democratic Republic abundantly show that land redistributions in North Vietnam
have resulted in the creation of thousands of "atomized" land holdings which
are unable to nourish their owner -- not to speak of his family -- or to provide
a sizeable surplus for urban consumption or for the People's Army:

> Moreover, the reform has been carried out for more than 10,000
> hectares /24,000 acres/ of land. The number of benefiting farmers
> was 22,699. The land distributed was taken from 3,262 landowners. (16)

> In the province of Bac-Giang, northeast of Hanoi, in the three-months
> period preceding September, 1950, nearly 14,000 farmers were congre-
> gated to receive 3,500 hectares of land which had formerly belonged
> to the traitors and imperialists. (17)

Taking the above-cited average yield figures as a basis of calculation, an
average farmers' family of four would thus require four acres of land in order
to survive -- without taking into account the taxes which it would have to pay
under the Republican tax law.

According to the two examples cited, the recipients of the land reapportionment received, in the first case, 1.05 acres each; and in the second
case, 0.6 acres! It is, therefore, more than doubtful that the land hunger
of the Vietnamese farmer, particularly in the extremely densely populated
regions of the Red River Delta, will have found relief in the measures taken
on his behalf by the Democratic Republic. It is more than likely that the
present state of the Republican agrarian policy follows the theme which has
been so eloquently defined by V. I. Lenin in his reply to Kautsky's accusation
that he had deviated from true Marxism by maintaining and even developing a
system of minute private landholdings:

> The proletarians tell the peasants: we shall help you to realize
> your desires in the direction of an ideal capitalism -- for an

equalitarian redistribution of landed property is nothing but an
idealization of capitalism from the point of view of the small-holder.
At the same time we shall demonstrate to you the impossibility of such
a system and the necessity to pass on to the collective culture of
land. (18)

Comments made on the same phase of agrarian reform in the Eastern European
satellites strike a familiar ring to anyone acquainted with Vietnamese villages
recently re-occupied by French Union or Vietnam National Forces after years of
Republican administration:

One could foresee that the immediate effect of the parcellization
of land...would have grave repercussions upon the agrarian production
and supply /situation/... Furthermore, the reform has increased the
number of 'minute holdings.' The allotted land is on the average...
hardly sufficient to nourish a family, particularly one of the large
Eastern European families. It has created frightening problems, such
as the installation of housing for the new landowners...
What a sorrowful and yet touching scene: those thousands of huts made
with scraps...inhabited by gaunt men and women, dressed in rags,
surrounded by a whole flock of children of all ages, men and women
whose faces reflect many contradictory feelings: pride of the new
owner, worry of the future, hope and despair...
The reform of 1944-45 has resolved but two aspects of the problem of
the rural East: the national and the social aspects. The economic
problem of agricultural organization remains unsolved. (19)

The problem could have hardly been couched in more accurate terms had the text
applied specifically to the Democratic Republic of Vietnam. It took the
Republican Government two years to realize fully the effects of the first set
of reforms. In 1952 began the second series of agricultural decrees which
seems to have found its culmination in the ratification of the final land
reform law by a hastily-reconvened National Assembly in December, 1953.

5. The Final Reforms.

As in the previous group of reforms, it is the seemingly secondary final
decree on land reapportionment which in fact contains the most important changes
in land tenure. A new "Provisional Statute concerning the Distribution of
Rice Fields and Communal Lands" was enacted by the Government in the form of
a decree (20), abrogating all prior legislation on the subject (21). On the
whole, the statute is strangely reminiscent of the Soviet "Land Decree" of
May 22, 1922, in that it attempts to regulate a transitional stage rather
than to prepare a final mold for a permanent new system of land tenure.

In its preamble, the new Decree states:

Since the victory of August /1945/, many changes have been made
concerning the distribution of rice land. In view of a more
appropriate application of the apportionment during the Resistance
/period/, the Government decides to enact the following statutes: (22)

In its General Principles, the order of priority of the distribution
criteria definitely reflects the state of war under which the statutes were
enacted:

- Increase of production;
- Reinforcement of the union of all land-toilers;
- Democracy and justice. (23)

The second important point in the Decree is the fact that the century-old practice of communal lands seems to be abolished, since under Chapter II, Article 2,

> Rice and Communal Lands will be distributed among the people, to all men and women over 16... Orphans under 16 will receive a part equivalent to one-third /of that/ of an adult.

Distribution may be made at village level, or centralized at huyen or inter-village level, if such a measure would guarantee a more equal distribution of the land.

At the same time, the Republican Government limited the maximum individual share to 0.5 hectare, a surface which may be deemed sufficient -- under optimum conditions -- of feeding its owner and paying the present-level agricultural taxes (Article 5). It also fully realized that there would not be a sufficient amount of land to satisfy the general demand, and set up a system of priority categories which includes the same groups that have benefited from previous reapportionments as well as from tax rebates or exemptions: the war veterans, families of killed soldiers, members of the guerilla forces, etc. (Article 7):

> They will receive the best part of the rice lands, superior to the others...

They are also among the favored group to be the first to receive land in the case of villages where there is too little available land to be distributed among all the needy peasants.

However, the core of the whole decree seems to be the fact that, under Article 8 and 9, which provide for up to 20% of the land given to farmers to be cultivated for the communal treasury, there is also set up a land-use rotation system for distributed communal lands, to be carried out every 3 to 5 years. In the case of death of a beneficiary, his next-of-kin may retain his share until the end of the calendar year (in practice, however, until the end of the harvest of the then standing crop). Thereafter, the land returns to the village for distribution to the next applicant.

Article 11 is interesting inasmuch as it constitutes a subtle attempt to break down religious beliefs by providing for the distribution of "rice lands used for the cult of genii and gods." Similar provisions, abolishing the land reserved for religious cults, may be found in other land reforms carried out by Soviet satellites (24).

Chapter IV of the land redistribution decree concentrates on what is called "semi-public" or "semi-private" lands, e.g., lands which had once been part of the public domain but which had been alienated by the Vietnamese emperors to reward the services of particularly meritorious generals or warriors; or which had been given away by private persons for religious uses; or are untilled communal land (Article 15).

Chapter VI provides for the organization of a "Rice and Communal Lands Redistribution Commission" to be formed by the President or an authorized delegate
of the UBKC/HC; one representative of the Lien Viet Front; one delegate of
the Agriculture Executive Committee and one or two representatives of the
farmers of each village concerned. The approval by the People's Council and
UBKC of the village or huyen (depending upon which basis the redistribution
takes place) is required for the final implementation of the reform.

Finally, Chapter VII contains the very interesting provision that the
present statute does not apply to the Nam-Bo (South Vietnam), i.e., the area
which contains the bulk of the large estates where such a redistribution,
while of course hurting production, would have had the best chances of really
satisfying the individual farmers (25). The Nam-Bo was left free to "propose
its own particular statute to the Central Government." It is not known whether
it did, and if so, whether it was implemented. In any case, the problem is
largely rhetorical, since most of the Nam-Bo's rice lands are -- for the time
being -- under control of the Vietnam National Government.

The new statute, therefore, does not contain anything that had not been
implemented before, under one form or another; but it does constitute a solid
indication of present trends in the country. By now apportioning tracts of
land which reach bare survival levels, and by compelling the tenants or owners
to increase their levels of production under threat of confiscation, the
Viet-Minh has succeeded in creating on a non-compulsory basis a huge floating
labor reserve of landless peasants who are readily absorbed by the "War
Workers Units" (i.e., pack-carriers for the mobile chu-luc units), by the
war industries and mines, and by the Regular Army and guerilla forces. The
ensuing "Mass Mobilization Movement" is but a logical outgrowth of the new
farm situation.

A. The Agrarian Reform of May, 1953.

The Decree on Agrarian Policy of April 20, 1953 (26), as it was officially
called, was published on May 20, 1953. Again, the new decree did not in any
way shake the system of agrarian property as such, but merely consolidated the
gains obtained during the previous period. Interest rates which had been
lowered by 25% by virtue of the July, 1949, decree, were reduced by another
25% or more,

> so that after the reduction it does not amount to more than one-third
> of the crop. (27)

The new law also successfully circumvenes certain errors which can be found,
for example, in the land reform of the Vietnam National Government, by
stipulating that "no other rents can be collected" (Article 5), and that
under no circumstances "can rents be increased " (Article 6). Those
articles close the loophole which enables certain landowners in the National
areas to obey the law by decreasing their rent on land while at the same time
increasing their rent on farming implements and draft animals. Another loophole which is often used in the Nationalist areas where the National Land
Reform (28) Act is being implemented is the menace of cancellation of contract
exercised by the landlord upon the tenant unless the latter agrees to
substantial under-the-counter payments which often completely offset the
effect of the decrease of rent. Articles 14 to 16 of the Republican Land
Decree expressly forbid the landlord to cancel the contracts with his tenants
on such grounds and provide for adequate appeal authorities.

The second part concentrates again upon reducing the debt load of the peasantry. Article 17 completely and permanently wipes out debts and interest payments upon transactions dating to before the August, 1945, revolution; while Article 18 declares a moratorium upon all debts contracted by the usually preferred classes (People's Army soldiers, poor peasants, etc.) towards persons living in Franco-Nationalist territory. At the same time peasants who had incurred debts towards landowners within the Republican zone after the 1950 law saw their interest rates reduced by 18 to 20 per cent, and total interest payments are not to exceed the original capital. Those regulations, however, do not apply to loans between poor farmers or laborers, and to commercial and industrial loans (Article 21).

Articles 25 to 30 definitely confiscate all property belonging to French imperialists and Vietnamese traitors and to usurping, despotic landlords, and give definitive title of such lands to the landless peasants who have received nothing or little during the previous reapportionments, with the usual priorities going to the stalwarts of the regime.

Articles 31 through 33 implement the 1950 law on uncultivated land or land whose owners reside in the area under control of the National Government. Land of the latter is given to landless farmers who may till it without paying back rent, but the land will be returned to its rightful owners upon their return, unless they were found guilty of treason. Uncultivated land becomes state property after two rather than five years of abandonment or non-cultivation.

Finally, Articles 35 and 36 establish a new centralized organization for the application of the agrarian policy, the Agrarian Committee, chaired by the Prime Minister, and composed of the Minister of Agriculture, the Minister of the Interior, a delegate of the Lien-Viet Front, and two delegates of the National Peasant Liaison Committee. A similar organization was set up at various local levels, down to the villages, with members of the local UBKC/HC, the agrarian committees, and representatives of poor peasants and farm hand organizations.

Subsequent articles (the whole decree has 53 articles) deal with specific cases of ownership and tenure and do not generally affect the over-all aspect of the problem.

As can readily be seen from the above, the Republican Government has once more avoided an all-out showdown with the feudal landowners and other local equivalents of "kulaks," probably so as to forestall major production break-downs or even uprisings on its territory and also in order to be able to hold out an olive branch to the landowners who were still fence-sitting in the area controlled by the Vietnam National Government.

Still, the news of the "land reform" was given due publicity throughout the whole territory of Vietnam and of the countries of the Soviet bloc (29). The Republican radio stations broadcast enthusiastic reports stating that

> The living conditions of the farmers will improve and the farmers will enthusiastically increase production, serve the front, enlist in the Army... (30)

An Agrarian Labor Hero, Hong Hanh stated:

Formerly, under the yoke of the French imperialists and the feudal landowners, my family had to work the whole year without stopping and still we went hungry and had only torn clothes. Now, on the contrary, we have a house with a tiled roof, a paved courtyard and baskets full of paddy, a pigsty and many fowl, and my children can go to school.

And an old peasant woman from Dong Bam (Thay Nguyen Province) wrote Ho Chi Minh:

During the French domination, my children and I lacked rice to feed ourselves and clothes to clad us. My children had to rent out their services and I continued to live from day to day by collecting potatoes and by digging the ground for roots... At the end of 1952, the peasants began the struggle against dishonest and nasty landlords... it is thanks to you that we now have such an easy life and we shall never forget it... (31)

6. Latest Developments.

A. Labor Exchange Movements.

Thanks to Hoang Hanh, a Catholic emulation fighter and Labor Hero, and many other similar labor heroes, the Republican Government began to develop a "Program of Mutual Assistance" and "Labor Exchanges," which, in a primitive way, resembles the Motor Tractor Stations of the more advanced satellites:

Since the day of the beginning of the study movement of the Hero Hoang Hanh...the organization of the labor exchange...has been re-organized by the Agricultural Association according to the experiences from various other places and in line with local conditions.
Each cell is composed of eight or nine families of medium or poor farmers...
Each cell contains farmers that have buffaloes and others that do not so that there may be mutual help for production... The comment upon the work performance, the attribution of points, and the advance planning of work to be done...are carried out in accordance with the principles of democracy, union and mutual help... (32)

Similar Hoang Hanh cells, comparable to Stakhanovite groups in other People's Democracies, now flourish throughout the Democratic Republic, and collective tilling of the land has become accepted in some areas, particularly in the Thanh-Hoa. Labor competitions are frequent and the winners are awarded cash or rice prizes, and at National Congresses of Model Cadres and Emulation Fighters, the most meritorious among them receive the coveted title of Labor Hero. Thus, "following the examples of the U.S.S.R. and the People's Democracies," a certain Ngo Gia Kham had increased his production by 436% (33), while a girl, Nguyen Thi Xiem, had increased her production of delaying fuses by 437% (34). There exists even a "Hero of the Free War Workers" (i.e., the supply carriers) (35). While, as shown in the preceding sections, the Democratic Republic did not officially pursue a policy of abolition of the big estates, such a policy is nonetheless carried out at local level in a series of actions euphemistically called "Mass Mobilization Movement."

B. The Mass Mobilization Movement.

This term actually covers the anti-landlord activities familiar to
students of Soviet bloc affairs, with about the same end results for the landlords. As previously shown in the section on the Republican Judiciary (Part
III, Section 9), "trials" of such landlords are staged according to a pattern
similar to that used with great success in People's China. The Republican
radio reports such cases with considerable detail, as the story of "How and
why Nguyen Rieng, Emulation Fighter of the Lien-Khu V, made himself useful,"
shows:

> ...I then thought /of the fact/ that we had to work while they /the
> landowners/ fed themselves on meat and fish. All that misery came
> from the cruel exploitation which the landowners exerted on us...
> Animated by a deep hatred, I have put all my efforts at the service
> of the mobilization of the peasant class in favor of the struggle
> ahead. (36)

However, all was not mellow in the implementation of the mass mobilization
(i.e., kulak-liquidation) policy. As in the U.S.S.R. under similar circumstances
decades ago, or in the aftermath of the Second World War, so the local government and party organizations in Vietnam had slowly become divorced from the
country at large and had introverted the order of priorities set up by the
central planners of the Workers' Party and of the Republican Government. In
an editorial titled "Let us apply the agrarian policy in co-ordination with
production work," the quasi-official Nhan-Dan lashed out at the party cadres:

> Up until now, in general, the application of the agrarian policy
> of the /Lao Dong/ Party has favored the interests of the peasants.
> However, in several regions, the cadres have still not understood
> that the essential aim of the agrarian policy was the development
> of production...they have failed to co-ordinate it with the mobilization
> of the masses in accordance with the line traced by the Party and
> Government. This attitude has damaged production development.

Likewise, some of the local Party groups indulged in a kind of land-grab which
had given a certain amount of trouble in the Ukrainian S.S.R. in the period
between 1946 and 1949.

> ...Cadres have only worried about taking...rice fields and thirty
> buffaloes as an 'autonomous fund' for the regional troops. The
> season has passed and the land has remained uncultivated.

In other areas, farmers were apparently forced to join collective farms,
which they were highly reluctant to do -- again with poor results for the
production.

> In certain regions the plantations /belonging to Frenchmen or
> Nationalists/ were only split among the collective farms (as in the
> case of Nghe An). Elsewhere...haste was made in grouping the farmers
> into collectives, without giving them the time to adjust their
> consciences so as to become volunteers. The farmers, feeling forced
> to join the collectives, have shown no enthusiasm in the service of
> production.

One other drawback of the land reapportionment policy was that the farmer who knew that he was about to obtain a better piece of farmland (or conversely, the landowner who knew that he was about to lose all of his) hardly did any field work but waited for events to develop.

> Many just replanted a little or only pretended they had done so, being afraid that their fields would be subject to redistribution while replanting was under way. (37)

There can be no doubt to the fact that the crisis had been serious, and this may be one of the reasons why the Republicans convened the full National Assembly -- after a lapse of more than six years -- merely to ratify the decrees on agrarian reform so as to give them force of law.

The whole kulak-expropriation (and extermination) machinery ground to a temporary halt during September, 1953, and on September 22, 1953, the Central Executive Committee of the Lao Dong Party issued its new "Directive on Mass Mobilization and its New Relations with the Rich Farmers" over the Republican radio network. The broadcast was a complete statement concerning "the policy towards the rich peasant":

> The common policy of the Party in the mobilization of the masses... previously consisted in basing itself upon the poor and landless peasants.. The policy which is imperative at present is the following: to base oneself upon the poor and landless peasants; to unite closely with the middle class peasants; to ally oneself with the rich peasants and to overthrow the reactionary Vietnamese traitors...
>
> Why ally ourselves with the rich peasants? Because the rich peasants at present participate in the struggle against the imperialists ...and it is necessary for us to concentrate all our forces upon overthrowing the imperialists and feudal /landlords7... Our present policy regarding the rich peasants consists in:
> a) on the political plane, allying ourselves with the rich peasants and in not entering into a struggle with them;
> b) on the economic plane, in respecting the resources of the rich farmers and in not touching them, and in leaving them free to hire labor. (38)

The meaning of this message of the Central Executive Committee of the Lao Dong Party is clear and unequivocal, and its effects were felt almost immediately. Most derogatory epithets were dropped in radio dispatches and press releases when the passage referred to the rich peasants. Accusations of murders, rapes, slavery and other crimes were limited to the "traitors" and "imperialists" from now on.

C. Conclusions.

Up to a certain point, the Democratic Republic has carried out agrarian reforms which were based on a realistic appraisal of the situation within its territory. Strong action tending to reduce usury and high land rent has beyond a doubt been a step in the right direction. On the other hand, by rigidly following a land distribution policy which was definitely not designed for the prevailing land distribution pattern and the mode of agricultural production in the areas under Republican control, the Democratic Republic found itself in the dilemma of having to deviate from either its economic or its doctrinary objectives. It chose -- for obvious reasons of survival -- deviation from the latter. However, this may be only a very temporary measure and there are some recent indications (39) that the anti-kulak trend has been fully resumed.

D. The December Conferences.

Without prior announcements, during the month of December, 1953, the National Assembly of the Democratic Republic met in plenary sessions as did the Central Executive Committee of the Lao Dong Party, and the National Conference of the Delegates of the Lao Dong Party.

It was the third session of the Assembly -- the two others having taken place in 1946 -- and 171 out of 444 original members were able to attend the meeting. They

> carefully studied and put up lively discussions on the bill of agrarian reforms to put into effect the slogan 'Land to the Tillers' ...In an atmosphere of great enthusiasm, the National Assembly unanimously sanctioned the Government's bill of agrarian reform... all the parliament members stood up and cheered President Ho Chi Minh with loud and prolonged applause and sang in chorus the 'Praise Ho Chi Minh' song... (40)

The discussion of the agrarian reform bill appears to have been a more serious affair at the Central Executive Committee of the Lao Dong, and the nearly month-long sessions of the first National Conference of the Lao Dong delegates, and the resolution which emerged from their meetings, while less sanguine than the one adopted by the Parliament, is probably much nearer to actual conditions:

> the land reform will be carried out gradually and cautiously and according to a well-prepared plan... (41)

What then have been the actual accomplishments of the land reform of the Democratic Republic? The major accomplishments appear to have been in the field of a more equal share of profits between the small farmer and the big landholder -- accompanied by an equally heavier burden of State on both. However, some figures were recently published by the Republican Government which may give an idea of what exactly has been done in the field of re-apportioning of the available land:

> Up to the end of 1952, the following achievements have been recorded:
> - 250,000 hectares of land have been provisionally allocated to nearly half a million peasants;
> According to still incomplete figures recorded in 1950, 344,373 farmers cultivated 150,915 hectares of land.
> According to still incomplete figures recorded in 1950, 317,000 hectares of communal land have been allocated to the labouring peasants in the free zones...
> The reduction of interest rates has been partly realized... (42)

Therefore, in 1950, some 344,000 farmers tilled a plot of 0.96 acres each. As we have seen previously, such a plot is notoriously too small even to assure the survival of the farmer himself, without leaving a surplus for his family, taxes or for non-agrarian consumption.

Two years later, the reapportioning of abandoned lands and of property belonging to Frenchmen and Vietnamese nationalists had added but a half hectare (1.2 acres) to the average farm, but the total number of farmers appears to have increased from 344,373 in 1950 to about a half-million in 1952. The individual apportionment of the communal lands yielded another 1.2 acres per farmer in the Republican zone (according to figures given above), so that the theoretical average holding of a farmer in the Republican zone might amount now to approximately 3.4 acres. However, some considerable restrictions must be placed upon the above figures. They include, of course, only the farmers lucky enough to receive anything at all, for the area under control of the Republican Government contains between eleven to thirteen million people, 90 per cent of whom are engaged in agricultural pursuits. Therefore—— and this was to be foreseen—— the Democratic Government could not possibly succeed in achieving a large-scale implementation of its own agrarian policy.

The Mass Mobilization Movement of the Peasantry, which had been founded early in 1953 with the aim of

> actively replenishing the peasant forces...to overthrow the reactionary feudal collaborationists and rural despots...

began by a first drive in the spring of 1953 which resulted in the application of anti-kulak measures in "22 test villages during this first drive."

> In September, 1953, the Vietnam Lao Dong Party and the People's Government (43) initiated the second mass mobilization drive in nearly 200 villages...a general review of its results is now on the way to completion. The forthcoming third drive will be carried out on a larger scale. (44)

E. The "Third Phase"

In fact, the "Third Phase" began almost at once, heralded by a long speech of Truong Chinh, the Secretary-General of the Vietnam Workers' Party, to the party delegates attending the first National Congress of the Vietnam Workers' Party, late in 1953 (45).

This phase of the movement means the full application of the land reform program under the old Soviet principle of "Land to the Tillers," and does not, in fact, show any radically new ideas. The army and other old favorites of the party receive the usual preferential treatment, but churches and other places of worship are not now totally deprived of their agricultural holdings (46).

An unconcealed appeal to desertion is made in favor of the Vietnamese who have cast their lot with the Franco-Nationalist side:

> The individual rebels (soldiers and non-commissioned officers) are entitled to a share in the lands which have been put aside for them. Such lands shall be temporarily administered by the regional authorities.
> Likewise, employees of the /Bao Dai/ administration who, upon their return to the free zones /i.e., Viet-Minh-controlled territory/ have insufficient means of livelihood, shall receive their quota of land, if they so desire. (47)

The "democratic personalities" among the landlords apparently will continue to enjoy, for the time being, the relief given them during the second phase of the land reform drive. Moreover, even the "traitorous, reactionary and cruel" landlords shall only be punished on an individual basis, while their families shall allegedly continue to receive their share of land. Under the new law, aliens shall be able to work a full share of land but shall not receive title to it.

The only conspicuous difference between this "Third Phase" of the Viet-Minh land reform and the other land reforms in the People's Democracies is that several stages of it co-exist not only in time but also in terms of geography. Truong Chinh repeatedly insists upon the fact that:

> Mass mobilization must precede the application of the Agrarian Reform. (48)

In fact, the whole second (and major) part of his speech deals with the practical application of the "Third Phase" in fringe areas or in areas which were only recently occupied by Viet-Minh forces and in which "Mass Mobilization," i.e., the ideological preparation for the liquidation of the landlords, has not yet taken deep roots:

> The agrarian reform is a struggle of classes which shall be pursued with vigor, without letting oneself be stopped by any difficulty... it is impossible to proceed with the agrarian reform by using merely peaceful means. Hence, the necessity to have recourse to propaganda. It is necessary to educate the popular masses, to jar them out of the torpor in which they wallow, to bring them to the point of rising up and entering into the struggle against the landlord class... The propaganda campaign which we have recently conducted in favor of the reduction of land rent has given us precious information, of which we shall make full use. (49)

The full application of Marxist dialectics in the implementation of the land reform is now fully apparent:

> Let us not forget that in the past, whenever a social class was on the verge of disappearing, it has always reacted with violence, using all fair and foul means at its disposal, in order to escape its impending fate.

However, the burden of the mass mobilization work is now shifted from the Vietnam Workers' Party to the Congresses of Peasant Delegates and the various local groups of the Agricultural Associations, which, as member organizations of the Lien-Viet Front, "shall execute policy as directed by the Party and the Government." The tactics to be used in order to prepare the political and psychological terrain for the "Third Phase" are explained in great detail:

2. Dismemberment of the landowning class and concentration of all anti-feudal forces so as to mobilize the masses. (50)

> The objective of our struggle is the suppression of the class of feudal landlords. In order to eliminate it for good, we must isolate it and progressively dismember it...

During the application of the land reform, the landlords who are considered as traitors...shall be immediately punished and brought before a Special People's Tribunal to be judged and to receive stringent punishment.

Chinh, therefore, cautions his cadres against the application of the "Third Phase" in areas which have not been submitted to a sufficiently intensive "mass mobilization," and names three major conditions which must be fulfilled before the reform can be fully applied:

a. A stabilized political and military situation;

b. Desire of a majority of the peasants to have the agrarian reform applied in their village;

c. Sufficient availability of guiding cadres;

adding that

Only the liberated regions can fulfill those three conditions; that is why one shall first of all undertake the agrarian reform in those regions. Generally speaking, guerilla zones do not fulfill those conditions. (51)

From the foregoing, it appears quite clearly that the clause respecting the "desire of the peasant" for or against the land reforms is somewhat symbolical, for in the following section, entitled: "The mass mobilization must be carried out methodically, progressively and regularly" (52), Chinh admonished his cadres as follows:

Do not believe that the mass mobilization permits us to do whatever the mass wants... The fact of unleashing the mass mobilization does not mean that all freedom shall be left to the cadres and to the population to follow their own good pleasure and to act according to their own free will; or not to follow the plan of the Central Government, or not to obey the orders and directives thus given...

The Central Executive Committee /of the Lao Dong Party/ shall follow a well-defined plan whose execution shall be implemented in several stages... That is why the cadres, as well as the popular masses, shall not show impatience and shall not implement the agrarian reform according to their own whim.

Therefore, the regions which have not received...the authorization to mobilize the popular masses to carry out the agrarian reform are absolutely forbidden to do anything at all in that direction. (53)

While the timing of the program itself is thus quite flexible, its application -- once decided upon -- is submitted to a type of unswerving rigidity which cannot augur too well for the success of its implementation. Indeed, recent reports from areas that now have been under Viet-Minh control for several years show that resistance against the new land reform is quite strong, particularly in the mountain areas where the Vietnamese are in a minority and where good political cadres are scarce:

Our efforts to carry out the mass mobilization successfully have met with numerous difficulties. Their political impact was severely shaken

in the course of the two preceding stages of the mass mobilization.
The landlords have multiplied their efforts of sabotaging it by new
methods...
    After the departure of the mobilization teams (54), those land-
lords have again taken up their intimidation maneuvers and during
the night went to the loyal farmers to menace them... (55)

The same report also mentions that the various ethnic minorities (Tho,
Man, Thai, etc.) view with distrust the Vietnamese intruders from the lowlands,
and that "several reactionary organizations and nests" had been discovered.

It is doubtless true that the ulterior motives of the Viet-Minh's land
reform are, for the time being, political, and not so much directed toward
its own thinly-populated hinterland, as to the teeming millions of land-
hungry peasants and debt-ridden tenants who till the extensive holdings of
landlords and rich farmers in areas under control of the Vietnamese Nationalist
Government.

It might very well be that ultimate victory in Indochina shall belong to
the side which can first make good its promises to better the dismally low
living standards of the rice farmer.

7. Summation.

This study has attempted to show how the Democratic Republic of Vietnam
developed in the aftermath of the Second World War upon the ruins of the French
colonial administration, and how it has successfully enforced its control
over an important portion of the territory and population of Vietnam.

After a hopeful beginning of constitutional democratic government, a
single party gained control of the state apparatus, the armed forces and the
bulk of the local administrative machinery. This party -- a direct successor
of the Indochinese Communist Party -- has successfully consolidated its grip
upon the State so that today the acts and policies of the Democratic Republic
closely resemble those of any other state of the Soviet orbit. This does
not mean that the Democratic Republic has abandoned its national objectives,
particularly as regards its regional aim of supremacy over the other member
states of the former Indochinese Federation.

It cannot be denied that the Viet-Minh -- as it is inaccurately called --
has long since passed the stage of a "guerilla government" which many Western
sources still think it is. Despite gravest odds, it fulfills all the
prerogatives of organized government -- including, indeed, a plethora of
bureaucratism -- over an area of more than 100,000 square miles, and has been
recognized by several members of the community of nations.

Thus, the D.R.V.N. is a State -- but a totalitarian state, for by no
stretch of the imagination can the regime that at present rules the Republican
zone be called "democratic" in the sense generally attributed to the term,
unless autocritiques, "brain-washing," show trials, one-party rule, supremacy
of a political party over the governmental machinery, are accepted as part of
the system.

Yet, it is true beyond a doubt that the Ho Chi Minh Government commands
the obedience, if not the affectionate loyalty, of the majority of the

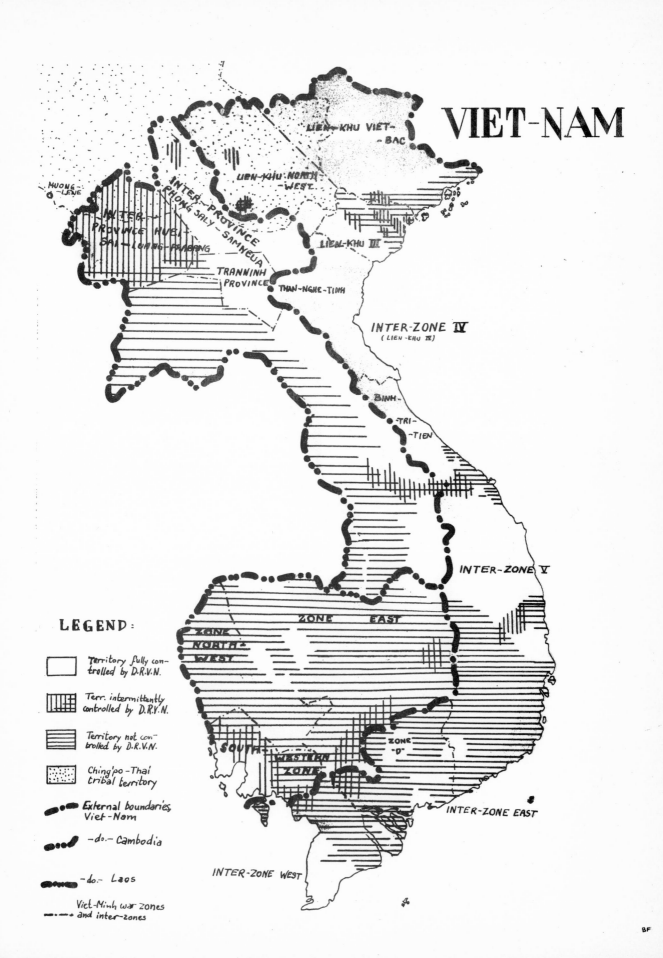

VIET-NAM

LIEN-KHU VIET-
-BAC

LIEN-KHU NORTH-
-WEST

MUONG-
-LENE

INTER-
PROVINCE
PHONG SALY-SAMNEUA

INTER-
PROVINCE HUE-
SAI-LUANG-PRABANG

LIEN-KHU III

TRANNINH
PROVINCE

THAN-NGHE-TINH

INTER-ZONE IV
(LIEN-KHU IV)

BINH-
-TRI-
-TIEN

INTER-ZONE V

ZONE   EAST

ZONE
NORTH-
WEST

ZONE
"D"

SOUTH-
WESTERN
ZONE

INTER-ZONE EAST

INTER-ZONE WEST

LEGEND:

Territory fully con-
trolled by D.R.V.N.

Terr. intermittently
controlled by D.R.V.N.

Territory not con-
trolled by D.R.V.N.

Chingpo-Thai
tribal territory

External boundaries
Viet-Nam

-do.- Cambodia

-do.- Laos

Viet-Minh war zones
and inter-zones

BF

Vietnamese (see Map 4). Does this mean that the Vietnamese are inclined to prefer a Communist-dominated regime to a Western-type democracy? Far from it. After more than seven years of hard jungle war, the Viet-Minh still faces serious morale and material problems, like any other state engaged in a drawn-out struggle -- even though its victorious conclusion is now clearly in sight. Until the recent disasters of Dien-Bien-Phu and of the Red River Delta, there were many thousands, members of the armed forces of the Republic or merely plain farmers, workers and intellectuals who cross the battle lines to seek a safe haven in the territory under control of the French and Vietnam National Forces. However, in a majority of 75 per cent they do so not because they have lost faith in the Republican Government, but merely because material living conditions are better in the Franco-Nationalist areas (56). Many line-crossers, while admittedly relieved to be out of the zone of control of the Republican Government, still profess admiration for the achievements and the men of the regime:

> The...personnel at any level leads a very strenuous life. It gets just enough /money/ to eat but not enough to clothe itself, and still its morale is good... The faithful and tenacious elements have very good morale; those whose morale is not so solid are severely criticized. (57)

Thus, the most likely reason for the popularity of the Republican regime is still the fact that the "other side," the camp of Western democracy as represented by the present Vietnam National Government, has thus far failed to offer a tangible alternative to the imagination-catching slogans and the effective grass-root reforms of the Viet-Minh.

Terms such as "Independence," "Resistance," "Land to the Tillers" have remained the apanage of the jungle fighters of the so-called Democratic Republic of Vietnam. And in the words of the late Marshal of France Jean De Lattre de Tassigny, "...there are individuals among them who fight very well for a very bad cause..." (58).

FOOTNOTES

1. U.S. Department of Agriculture, The Agriculture of Indochina (mimeo.), Washington, 1950, pp. 5-6. Figures adjusted for increase of population.

2. One mau is 0.89 acres in North Vietnam and 1.24 acres in Central Vietnam. One hectare (10,000 m^2) is 2.4 acres.

3. op. cit., p. 11.

4. Ibid., p. 11.

5. A fact which did not preclude the existence of some very large estates in the north, too, such as the 12,500-acre Tartarin estate in Bacgiang.

6. Op. cit., p. 1.

7. D.R.V.N., The Manifesto and Platform of the Vietnam Lao Dong Party (Engl.), op. cit., Article 6, p. 8.

8. D.R.V.N., Agrarian Policy in Viet-Nam (mimeo.), 1952, p. 6.

9. D.R.V.N., Decree No. 25/FL of 19 February, 1950.

10. Agrarian Policy in Viet-Nam, op. cit., p. 8.

11. Parenthesis in text.

12. See also pp. 91-92 on agrarian taxation.

13. Radio Voice of Vietnam, February 26, 1951.

14. Nhan-Dan (daily), No. 115, June 6, 1953.

15. U.S. Department of Agriculture, op. cit., p. 24. Other typical acreage yields are: 3,408 in Japan, 2,295 in Korea and 2,259 lbs./acre in China. On the other hand, Indochina has the third-highest per-capita production.

16. Radio Voice of Vietnam, December 15, 1950.

17. D.R.V.N., Viet-Nam Information Agency, Release of January 8, 1951.

18. Lenin, V. I., "La Révolution prolétarienne et le renégat Kautsky," in Oeuvres Choisies (French Ed.), Vol. VII, p. 201.

19. Fejtö, François, Histoire des Democraties Populaires, Editions Du Seuil, Paris, 1952, pp. 150-151.

20. D.R.V.N., No. 87/SL of May 5, 1952, published in Cu'u Quoc (daily), No. 2076 of December 10, 1952.

21. Article 2 of Implementing Decree.

22. D.R.V.N., No. 87/SL, op. cit.

23. Ibid., Chapter I, Article 1.

24. Article 3(d) of the land reform decree of March 5, 1946, of the North Korean People's Republic limits such confiscation of religious property to lands above 5 hectares -- a notable exception in the Soviet orbit, which the Viet-Minh appears to have followed later on (see Section 6(E) below).

25. Article 22, Chapter VII.

26. D.R.V.N., Decree No. 149/SL of April 20, 1953, transmitted over Radio Voice of Vietnam, May 20, 1953.

27. Op. cit., Article 3.

28. State of Vietnam, Bo Luat Dien-Dia (Agrarian Code), Ordinances 19 to 22 of June 4, 1953.

29. Hsinhua News Agency, Bulletins, 21, 22, 23 and 26 May 1953.

30. D.R.V.N., Radio Voice of Vietnam, May 22, 1953.

31. D.R.V.N., Radio Voice of Bac-Bo, Information Service Lien-Khu III, June 4, 1953.

32. D.R.V.N., Radio Voice of Vietnam, June 6, 1953.

33. Ibid., June 27, 1951.

34. Id., February 10, 1951.

35. Id., July 20, 1951.

36. Id., Lien-Khu V, September 17, 1953.

37. Nhan Dan (daily), No. 127, of September 7, 1953.

38. Voice of Vietnam, September 22, 1953. Italics in original text.

39. New York Times, January 8, 1954. However, the reporter may be confusing the kulaks with the feudal landlords and "traitors," against whom the Viet-Minh never relented.

40. D.R.V.N., Vietnam Information (Bulletin), No. 52/53 of December 31, 1953, p. 2.

41. Ibid., p. 3. Italics mine.

42. Ibid., p. 6.

43. This appears to be the first instance in which the Democratic Republic referred to itself as a People's Government.

44. Ibid., p. 7.

45. D.R.V.N., Vietnam Information Agency (Morse Report), February 23, 1954.

46. Ibid., Section 1, Article 2, (d).

47. _Id._, Article 2(e).

48. _Ibid._, Title of Section II.

49. _Id._, Section II, Article 1.

50. Italics in the original text.

51. Section II, Article 4.

52. Section II, Article 5, italics in original text.

53. _Ibid._, end of speech.

54. See Part Three, p. 44.

55. D.R.V.N., _Vietnam Information Agency_, North Vietnam, Broadcast of March 26, 1954.

56. The writer personally made a statistical survey of the persons who had crossed the lines in North Vietnam during the first six months of 1953. Of the total, one-third were People's Army personnel, 20% coolies and landless peasants and 7% members of liberal professions. 10% were purged, 38% came over because life was too hard and only 9.5% professed to be anti-Viet-Minh.

57. High Commissioner of France in Indochina, French Security Service in North Vietnam, _Report_ of July 17, 1953.

58. High Commissioner of France in Indochina, _A Call to Vietnamese Youth_ (printed pamphlet), Speech by Marshal de Lattre de Tassigny at the Graduation Ceremonies of the Lycee Chasseloup-Laubat, Saigon, 1951, p. 13.

APPENDIX I

THE CONSTITUTION

OF THE DEMOCRATIC REPUBLIC

OF VIETNAM

Adopted by the National Assembly by a vote of 240 to 2 at its meeting on November 8th, 1946, in Hanoi, capital of the Democratic Republic of Vietnam, and proclaimed on November 9th, 1946.

PREAMBLE

The August Revolution regained the independence of our Fatherland and the liberty of our people, and founded the Democratic Republic.

After 80 years of struggle, the Vietnamese people threw off the colonial yoke and, at the same time, abolished the internal feudal regime.

The nation entered upon a new stage in its history.

From now on our people face the tasks of preserving the integrity of our territory, achieving full independence and building up the country on democratic foundations.

Being entrusted by the nation with the task of drafting the first Constitution of the Democratic Republic of Vietnam, the National Assembly is deeply conscious that the Constitution, to embody the glorious achievements of the Revolution, should be based on the following principles:

The union of all the people without distinction of race, class, creed, wealth or sex;

The guarantee of democratic liberties;

The establishment of a true people's government.

Permeated by the spirit of unity symbolized in the struggle of the entire nation and manifested in an enlarged and enlightened democratic regime, Vietnam now goes forward confidently in consonance with the progressive movements of the world and the peaceful aspirations of mankind.

CHAPTER I

GENERAL PROVISIONS

1. Vietnam is a Democratic Republic.
All power in the country belongs to the people of Vietnam without distinction of race, class, creed, wealth or sex.

2. The territory of Vietnam, composed of Bac-Bo or Northern Vietnam, Trung-Bo or Central Vietnam, and Nam-Bo or Southern Vietnam, is one and indivisible.

3. The national flag of Vietnam is red, centered with a five-pointed golden star.

The national anthem of Vietnam is the "Tien Quan Ca."

The Capital of Vietnam is Hanoi.

CHAPTER II

THE DUTIES AND RIGHTS OF THE CITIZENS

A. - DUTIES.

4. It is the duty of every citizen:
- to defend the country;
- to abide by the Constitution;
- to observe the laws.

5. All Vietnamese citizens are liable for military service.

B. - RIGHTS.

6. All Vietnamese citizens enjoy equal rights in the economic, political and cultural fields.

7. All Vietnamese citizens are equal before the law and enjoy equal opportunity to participate in the administration and in national construction, each according to his or her abilities and character.

8. Besides enjoying full and equal rights, ethnic minorities are to receive every help and encouragement to enable them to reach the common level of advancement as speedily as possible.

9. Women enjoy full and equal rights with men under the Constitution in every respect.

10. Vietnamese citizens enjoy:
- Freedom of speech,
- Freedom of the press,
- Freedom of assembly and meeting,
- Freedom of religion,
- Freedom to reside and travel in the country or to go abroad.

11. Vietnamese citizens may not be arrested and detained except under the law, and their residence and correspondence are inviolable.

12. The rights of property and possession of Vietnamese citizens are guaranteed.

13. The rights and interests of both manual and intellectual workers are guaranteed.

14. Aged and infirm Vietnamese citizens unfit to work are to be assisted by the state. And the education of children is to be provided for.

Primary education is compulsory and free of charge. In local primary schools, ethnic minorities have the right to learn in their own language.

Poor students are to be helped by the government. Private schools are free to operate; they have to conform to the educational program provided by the Government.

Foreigners who immigrate owing to their struggle for Democracy and Freedom are granted the right of asylum in Vietnam.

C. - ELECTION - REVOCATION - VETO.

17. The mode of elections to all popular representative state bodies is first and primarily through universal suffrage by free, direct and secret ballot.

18. All Vietnamese citizens from the age of 18 upwards, without distinction of sex, have the right to vote, except lunatics and those deprived of civic rights.

Candidates must be qualified electors, at least 21 years of age, and must be able to read and write the Vietnamese language. Citizens on military duty have the right to vote and to stand for elections on a par with all other citizens.

19. The method and procedure of polling is to be determined by law.

20. All citizens have the right to recall their elected representatives according to Articles 41 and 61.

21. All citizens have the right to decide on constitutional issues and all problems affecting the destiny of the nation according to Articles 32 and 70.

CHAPTER III

THE PEOPLE'S PARLIAMENT

22. The People's Parliament is the body entrusted with supreme powers in the Democratic Republic of Vietnam.

23. The People's Parliament decides all questions of common national interest such as the enactment of laws, the sanctioning of budgets and the ratification of agreements entered into with foreign countries.

24. Parliamentary elections are to be held normally once every three years, there being ordinarily one parliamentary representative for every 50,000 inhabitants.

The number of parliamentary representatives for up-country areas where there are ethnic minorities and for large cities will be determined by law.

25. A member of the People's Parliament represents not only his own constituency but the entire nation as well.

26. The People's Parliament determines if necessary on the validity of elections and accepts the resignation of its members.

27. The People's Parliament shall elect from its members its own President and two Vice-Presidents along with twelve permanent and three substitute members to form its Permanent Committee. The President and Vice-Presidents of the People's Parliament will assume the functions of Chairman and Vice-Chairman of the Permanent Committee respectively.

28. The People's Parliament shall meet twice a year on being convoked by the Permanent Committee (about May and December).

The Permanent Committee, when it deems necessary, may summon the People's Parliament to an extraordinary meeting.

The Permanent Committee shall summon the People's Parliament if at least a third of all the members of the latter so desire or if, in exceptional circumstances, the Government requires it to do so.

29. At every meeting of the People's Parliament at least half of its total membership shall constitute a quorum. To declare war, the decisions must be taken by at least a two-thirds majority.

30. The meeting of the People's Parliament is open to the public. The press is allowed to report all deliberations and decisions arrived at.

In exceptional cases, the People's Parliament is entitled to hold a secret meeting.

31. The President of the Democratic Republic of Vietnam shall promulgate all bills, measures and laws which have been passed by the People's Parliament not later than ten days after they have been voted upon. However, within this interval of time, the President of Vietnam may ask the People's Parliament to re-consider its decision. The President is under obligation to publish any revised decision of the People's Parliament.

32. Any matter vitally concerning the nation's destiny must be presented to the nation for final decision, if agreement by at least two-thirds of the People's Parliament has been obtained to this effect.

The mode of procedure for arriving at this final decision will be fixed by law.

33. The People's Parliament may dissolve itself with the consent of at least two-thirds of all its members. The Permanent Committee, in the name of the People's Parliament, shall proclaim such dissolution.

34. When the People's Parliament dissolves, whether the period of its normal duration be expired or not, its functions shall be assumed by the Permanent Committee until a new Parliament is elected.

35. Two months before the normal expiration of the People's Parliament, the Permanent Committee shall announce re-elections. These re-elections must be carried out within these two months before the expiration of the People's Parliament.

When the People's Parliament voluntarily dissolves, the Permanent Committee immediately proclaims re-elections. These re-elections must be carried out within two months after dissolution.

The Permanent Committee must convoke the new Parliament at the latest one month after elections.

If the term of office of the People's Parliament expires during such a crisis as time of war, the Permanent Committee is allowed to prolong their functioning for an indefinite time; however, the People's Parliament must be re-elected not later than six months after the end of such a crisis.

36. During the time that the People's Parliament does not meet, the Permanent Committee is entitled:

a) to vote on bills and decrees and other such projects proposed by the Government. All such decisions are to be presented to the People's Parliament at its next meeting, in order to get them approved, rescinded or modified;

b) to convoke the People's Parliament;

c) to control and criticize the Government.

37. To be valid and binding, all the Permanent Committee's decisions must be accepted by more than half of its members.

38. If the People's Parliament cannot meet, the Permanent Committee and the Government are together entitled to decide upon war or peace.

39. After the report of the Permanent Committee on its interim activities, which is to be presented at the beginning of every session, a vote of confidence in the Permanent Committee may be proposed, if requested by not less than a fourth part of the total members of the People's Parliament. In case of no-confidence, the whole Permanent Committee must resign.

Out-going members of the last Permanent Committee are eligible for re-election.

40. The Government may not ordinarily arrest or pass sentence on any of the members of the People's Parliament without the prior permission of the People's Parliament or, in case it is not meeting, of the Permanent Committee.

A member of the People's Parliament may not be prosecuted for a speech or opinion expressed during the sessions.

In case of flagrant breaches of the common laws, the Government may arrest a member of the People's Parliament, but it has to report to the Permanent Committee within twenty-four hours; the Permanent Committee or the People's Parliament will decide on the validity of such arrest.

When a member of the People's Parliament loses his right to vote, he loses at the same time all his rights and privileges as a member of the People's Parliament.

41. If the People's Parliament receives a request from at least a fourth part of the electors of any constituency to recall their parliamentary representative, it must consider the question. And if at least two-thirds of all the members of the People's Parliament agree to dismiss this parliamentary representative, he must resign.

42. The honorarium of the members of the People's Parliament will be determined by law.

CHAPTER IV

THE GOVERNMENT

43. The highest executive authority of the whole nation is the Government of the Democratic Republic of Vietnam.

44. The Government consists of the President of the Democratic Republic of Vietnam, the Vice-President and the Cabinet. The Cabinet consists of the Prime Minister, the other Ministers and Under-Secretaries and, if need be, a Deputy Prime Minister.

45. The President of the Democratic Republic of Vietnam is chosen from among the members of the People's Parliament and elected by a majority of at least two-thirds of all its members.

If, during the first vote, the requisite majority is not reached, the second vote shall decide by a relative majority. The President of Vietnam is elected for five years and may be re-elected for consecutive terms. One month before the expiration of his term, the Permanent Committee must summon the People's Parliament to elect a new President.

46. The Vice-President of Vietnam is elected by the People's Parliament in the same way as the President. The length of his tenure of office is the same as that of the People's Parliament.

The Vice-President assists the President. In case the President dies or resigns, the Vice-President temporarily replaces him. The new President must be elected subsequently within two months.

47. The President of Vietnam chooses the Prime Minister from the People's Parliament and presents his appointment to the People's Parliament for approval.

If the choice is approved by the People's Parliament, the new Prime Minister may nominate all the Ministers from among the People's Parliament and presents the nominated list to the People's Parliament for approval.

The Under-Secretaries may be chosen from outside the People's Parliament and must be introduced by the Prime Minister to the Government's Council for approval.

The members of the Permanent Committee are not allowed to participate in the Cabinet.

48. In case of a Ministerial vacancy, the Prime Minister, in agreement with the Permanent Committee, appoints immediately a temporary substitute pending approval by the People's Parliament.

49. The President of the Democratic Republic of Vietnam:
    a) represents the Nation;
    b) is invested with the command of the whole nation's armed forces, appoints or dismisses commanders of the land army, navy, and air forces;
    c) signs decrees appointing the Prime Minister, members of the Cabinet and high officials of the Government;

d) presides over the Government's Council;

e) promulgates all laws decided by the People's Parliament;

f) confers decorations or honorific diplomas;

g) decrees special amnesties;

h) signs agreements with foreign nations;

i) assigns representatives of Vietnam to foreign countries and receives foreign representatives;

j) declares war or peace according to Article 28.

50. The President of the Republic is above the law unless he betrays the nation.

51. In case the President, the Vice-President or a Cabinet member is prosecuted for treason, the People's Parliament will set up a special tribunal for his trial.

Arrest and legal prosecution of a member of the Cabinet for common law delinquencies must be previously agreed upon by the Government's Council.

52. The Government is empowered to:

a) execute laws and decrees of the People's Parliament;

b) propose bills or laws to the People's Parliament;

c) suggest emergency bills or laws to the Permanent Committee while the People's Parliament is not meeting;

d) annul orders and decisions of all subordinate administrative organs, if need be;

e) appoint or dismiss officials in its administrative organs and technical branches;

f) execute mobilization orders and take all measures required for national security;

g) draft and present the annual budget.

53. Every decree of the Government must bear the signature of the President of the Republic of Vietnam and the signatures of one or several other Ministers concerned as well.

These Ministers are responsible to the People's Parliament.

54. Any Minister, on a successful motion of no-confidence against him by the People's Parliament, must resign. The whole Cabinet is not jointly responsible for individual Ministers.

The Prime Minister is responsible for the Cabinet's policy. A no-confidence motion may be deliberated by the Parliament only when proposed by the Prime Minister, the Permanent Committee or a fourth part of the whole People's Parliament.

Within a space of 24 hours after the People's Parliament has passed a motion of no-confidence in the Cabinet, the President of the Republic is entitled to propose that the no-confidence motion be re-examined by the People's Parliament.

The second deliberation must be held, at the latest, 48 hours after the first one. Subject to the preceding qualification, the Cabinet must at once resign on a no-confidence motion being passed against it.

55. All Ministers have to answer, either orally or in writing, to all relevant questions of the People's Parliament or the Permanent Committee. At the latest they must answer within the space of ten days after receiving questions.

When the People's Parliament dissolves, whether its normal duration be expired or not, the Cabinet exercises power till a new People's Parliament meets.

CHAPTER V

PEOPLE'S COUNCIL AND ADMINISTRATIVE COMMITTEE

57. From the executive point of view, Vietnam comprises three main administrative units (bo), namely Northern, Central and Southern. Each bo is divided into provinces, provinces into (prefectures and) districts, and (prefectures and) districts into villages.

58. In each province and village there is a People's Council elected by direct universal suffrage.

These administrative units elect their own Administrative Committee.

In bo and districts (or prefectures), there are only Administrative Committees. A bo's Committee is elected by the People's Councils of its respective provinces and cities. District and prefectural Executive Committees are elected by their respective village and quarter People's Councils.

59. The People's Councils decide upon questions peculiar to their own localities. These decisions must not conflict with orders issued by higher authorities.

Committees must:
    a) carry out orders issued by higher authorities;
    b) execute decisions of their own People's Councils after these decisions have been approved by higher authorities;
    c) manage the administrative machinery in their own localities.

60. A Committee is responsible to higher authorities as well as to its own People's Council.

61. The members of People's Councils and Executive Committees may be compelled to resign; correct procedure for the purpose will be determined by law.

62. A Government Act will determine the details of the organization of People's Councils and Executive Committees.

CHAPTER VI

THE JUDICIARY ORGANS

63. The judiciary organs of Vietnam consist of:
    a) A Supreme Court of Appeals,
    b) Appeals Courts,
    c) Provincial and Prefectural Courts.

64. All judges are appointed by the Government.

65. All criminal cases must be attended by a People's Jury who either proffer advice, if the case be one of "misdemeanor," or give verdicts with the judge if the case be one of "felony."

66. The national minorities may use their own language before the Tribunal.

67. The trial sessions must be held in public unless extraordinary circumstances preclude such procedure. All accused are allowed to conduct their own defence or plead with the assistance of an advocate.

68. It is forbidden to torture, strike or ill-treat accused persons and prisoners.

69. While trying cases, the judges have to discharge their functions in conformity with the law. No other authority is allowed to interfere with the functions of the judiciary.

CHAPTER VII

AMENDMENT OF THE CONSTITUTION

70. Amendments to a part or to the whole of the Constitution are subject to the following conditions:

 a) the amendments must be requested by at least a two-thirds majority of the whole People's Parliament;

 b) the People's Parliament must elect a committee to draft the amendments;

 c) the amendments, when thus ratified by the People's Parliament, must be put before the whole nation for final approval.

APPENDIX II

ORGANIZATION OF A VILLAGE IN THE VIET-MINH ZONE

District of Tien Hai UBKC/HC   DEMOCRATIC REPUBLIC OF VIETNAM
 (Committee for Resistance and   Independence-Freedom-Happiness
  Administration)
- - - - - - - - - - - - - -
No. 800 /H.C./H.C.

REORGANIZATION OF THE ADMINISTRATIVE POWER
OF THE TOWNSHIPS (OR COMMUNES) OF THE FREE ZONE

I. THE U.B.K.C. OF THE COMMUNES

A. DISTRIBUTION OF PERSONALITIES

-The President assumes the direction of all matters and is responsible for them.

-The Vice-President permanently substitutes for the President and is responsible for maintaining order in the township.

-The Delegate Secretary takes care of the reports and of all the administrative paperwork of the township.

These three persons form the Judiciary Committee of the township.

-The "Financial" Delegate is in charge of expenditures of the township in paddy and of the distribution of rice belonging to the Government.

-The "Economic" Delegate assumes the direction of the village Cooperative and of the blockade of the enemy economy.

-The "Military" Delegate commands the popular troops and guerillas and organizes the guard service.

-A Delegate is entrusted with the inspection of the village, with the maintenance of roads, and with popular education of the town.

Such is the division of work within the village UBKC/HC. In fact, however, only three or four men are fully occupied by their share in the responsibilities: the President, the Vice-President and one or two Delegates. As to the other Delegates, either by their incompetence, or because they don't have the means, they have almost nothing to do (the financial, economic delegates...). Therefore, they must assume tasks other than their principal mission. Example: the Delegate entrusted with popular instruction should also be entrusted with the manpower problems of the town.

Besides the tasks of chief of the Popular Troops and guerillas of the commune, the Military Delegate must well understand that being a Delegate of the Committee, he must know what the other Delegates do and help them in their common task which is the development of guerilla warfare. It is preferable not to entrust this mission to the Military Delegate above, with complete liberty of action.

A continual understanding between the President, Vice-President and Secretary Delegate is necessary to adequately perform all these duties. They must give an account of their acts to the Delegates of the Committee at their meetings.

B. THE INSPECTION AND DIRECTION OF MATTERS CONCERNING EACH VILLAGE

Except for the President and the Military Delegate, all the other Delegates must each take charge of the affairs of one or several villages. The Secretary Delegate attends to those of the village where his office is installed; the Financial and Economic Delegates can each assume charge of several villages. According to their occupations, the Delegates will come to the seat of the Committee every day or once every two or three days to exchange their viewpoints and make up their reports in common.

At the close of these meetings, the circulars or instructions coming from the higher echelons or from the UBKC/HC of the town will be sent to the Committee of each village to be carried out. The responsible Delegate helps these Committees in all circumstances. He has the additional duty of following the developments of the Committees' activities which he reports to the UBKC/HC of the town. The latter must act in the best interests of the villages placed under its administration.

C. THE ORGANIZATION OF THE SECRETARY'S OFFICE

The President or the Vice-President or one of the Delegates receives the people in a permanent office which serves as the liaison office with the administrative organs of the province or district.

The papers and account books of the Secretary's Office can be classified into three categories: 1) Administrative, and 2) Judicial: kept by the Secretary Delegate; and 3) Financial: kept by the Financial and Economic Delegate. The President himself takes charge of the keeping of accounts of expenditures and receipts.

1) Administrative Papers:

    a) Incoming and outgoing mail.
    b) Calendar of events.
    c) Registry of work being performed.
    d) Registry of the minutes of the People's Council.
    e) Registry of the decisions of the Committee.
    f) Registry of the materials of the Secretary's Office and of public property.
    g) Records.
    h) Registry of the general directives.

2) Judicial Papers:

    a) Incoming and outgoing mail.
    b) Recording of petitions in penal and civil matters.
    c) Registry of police court cases.
    d) Registry of the Conciliation /Committee/.
    e) Registry of statutes to be implemented.

3) Financial Papers:

    a) Registry of expenditures (money, paddy).
    b) Registry of receipts.
    c) Expense vouchers.
    d) Subscription of bonds.
    e) Deductions of paddy.
    f) Registration.
    g) Cattle-slaughtering taxes.
    h) Licenses.
    i) Distribution of paddy.

The registers and papers concerning the budget of the Commune are certainly numerous. But it is important to keep them all well in order so as to facilitate the settlement of accounts with the people and with the higher authorities. In anticipation of the possible disappearance of these records, it is necessary to have an additional record for all the expenditures and receipts.

D. RELATIONS OF THE UBKC/HC OF THE TOWNSHIP WITH THE VARIOUS GROUPS AND SERVICES

Besides the meetings where the staff of these groups and services are present, there exist permanent relations between the UBKC/HC and these groups and services for the purpose of consolidating the popular power and acting in good agreement in all circumstances so as to achieve good results.

The UBKC/HC must know well and help in their particular tasks the staff of these various groups and services who must forward to the UBKC/HC a copy of all the reports addressed to the higher echelons.

II. THE VILLAGE COMMITTEE

Since August, 1950, and according to the importance of the villages, committees have been created, composed of three to five members, among whom are found the former chief of the village, the agent of the Information Services and the chief of the Popular Troops. This Committee could not furnish satisfactory work until now, since its members have not realized the importance of their mission: they acted separately without thinking of the common responsibility of the Committee. This mistaken conception is to be eliminated by the members of the Committee of the village, who must apply the procedure of work of the UBKC/HC of the township: collective authority and individual responsibility.

Division of Work:

The distribution of work must be very clear. If the Committee is composed of three persons, the Chairman of the Committee is responsible for the office, and, in general, controls all the work. The Deputy-Chairman replaces the Chairman during his absence, takes charge of the information work and of the liaison with the different groups and services of the village, while another member performs the duty of chief of the Popular Troops and guerillas. If the Committee is made up of five people, the fourth will take over popular instruction, and the last will take over the secretary's work from the Chairman of the Committee.

The members of the Committee must see each other every day to exchange viewpoints and meet three times a month around the 1st, 11th, and 21st. One of these three meetings must bring together representatives of the various groups, the chiefs of the hamlets, members of the Communal Council living in the village, and the member of the UBKC/HC of the township responsible for the village to this UBKC/HC.

The Committee will establish the program of the meeting upon the basis of instructions received from the higher echelons and in accordance with the work load of the village.

This Committee also has the task of guiding and directing the various groups and services functioning in the village.

Budget:

In order to establish a common budget for the entire township all the expenditures of the village must first of all be subjected to the approval of the township, with the exception of the allotment assigned to the members of the Committee, and all the receipts will be handled at the township treasury.

/District of/ TIEN HAI, December 29, 1951

UBKC/HC of Tien Hai

The President: VO NGOC TRAN

APPENDIX III

"THE ACHIEVEMENTS OF THE YEAR 1953 AND THE TASKS WHICH WE SHALL HAVE TO FULFILL
IN 1954"

(Editorial of the Vietnam Workers' Party Newspaper, Nhan Dan, No. 164 for the
week 6-10 February, 1954.)

/When compared with the previous annual programs, the accent put on
political indoctrination in every field is remarkable. Its effects should not
be underestimated. -- B.B.F./

- - - - - - - - - - -

A. Summary of the work accomplished in 1953

In 1953 our long-term resistance has shown notable progress. Numerous
realizations have illustrated the general upswing of our national movement. The
following achievements have been made:

1. Military reorganization and particularly politico-military action, which
has permitted our soldiers to make rapid progress and to accomplish numerous
feats of arms.

2. Political instruction has been a great success in 1953. It has raised
morale, the political level of education, the spirit of responsibility of the
organization of discipline of the cadres. It has had an excellent influence
upon the application of government directives and in the accomplishment of missions.

3. Mass mobilization to obtain the effective reduction of land rent has
been the principal mission of 1953...

4. In the field of economics and finance, an important task has been
accomplished in 1953, a task which had been set in 1951: the increase of the
receipts and the decrease of expenditures...

Important works have been carried out concerning roads and bridges.
There has been progress in the transport of supplies destined to the front
lines. Commercial exchanges with China have taken an upswing.

5. The struggle in the enemy rear areas has been strongly developed,
guerilla warfare has been strongly intensified... The propaganda against enemy
troops has been developed.

The military reorganization has permitted our army to develop from every
point of view. Political instruction guarantees the implementation of the
policy of the government and the accomplishment of all missions of resistance...

B. Action Program for 1954

In his report on the situation of the missions for accomplishment in
connection with agrarian reform, President Ho has indicated the principal tasks
to be accomplished this year: to exterminate the enemy and to implement the
agrarian reforms... Upon the basis of the instructions given by President Ho,
one can trace the following picture of the tasks to be accomplished in 1954:

<u>In the military field.</u>

Intensify our action tending to overthrow enemy maneuvers and win more victories. Consolidate and develop the popular troops in every facet of their action.

<u>Mobilization of the masses so as to implement the agrarian reforms.</u>

In 1954 the mass mobilization for the nation-wide decrease of land rents and for the implementation of agrarian reform in the regions where this is possible must be continued.

The Central Executive Bureau is in charge of directing agrarian reform and shall centralize the information furnished by the zones and provinces which control the rational decrease of the land rent. In the zones and provinces one must organize the mass mobilization so as to achieve that decrease. The overall direction of the movement must be enforced. The provinces must know the role of the Central Executive Bureau: it is in charge of unifying the general action of the cadres so that the mass mobilization can be carried out in an orderly fashion, rapidly, thoroughly and upon a solid basis, so as to save time while carrying out the task assigned by the government.

<u>Economy and finances.</u>

The methods to apply and the tasks to be accomplished are the following: Cooperation with the mass movement... Development of agricultural production and of family artisan enterprise... Forestry products, small industry, and production of foodstuffs. Accomplishment of missions concerning the construction of roads and bridges so as to facilitate the supply of the front lines... Intensify internal commerce, respect the forms of commerce as carried out in the regions populated by ethnic minorities...

<u>Social culture.</u>

As far as propaganda and political structures are concerned, one must carry out two principles: conduct educational propaganda in favor of national union for resistance, reconquest of real independence, and the safeguard of world peace; spread education on agrarian policy so that production is accelerated.

As far as cultural education is concerned, one must: put through a rational increase of educational levels where the mass mobilization for land rent reduction and for the application of agrarian reform has been initiated; give the masses useful objectives in the extension of culture and in the bettering of the quality of same.

<u>Public health.</u>

Practice "patriotic hygiene" to avoid illnesses. Destroy parasites. Watch the health of the population and particularly that of our compatriots living in enemy rear areas.

<u>The /National Union/ Front and the propaganda among the population.</u>

Consolidate and develop the National Union Front in the struggle against Imperialism; concentrate all anti-feudal forces; develop solidarity between various /ethnic/ populations and the sects of various religions.

Actively propagandize among the population; positively help the young people and women particularly.

The Friendship Associations "Vietnam-Soviet Union" and "Vietnam-China" must do their best to consolidate and to develop feelings of friendship for the peoples of the friendly countries.

Organization of the Party.

Implant cadres in the nationalized industries.

Educate for mass mobilization, form and build up cadres, strengthen their direction, better them in all fields...

On the subject of guidance:

Insure the implementation of all the tasks named above and particularly watch the following points:

In directing positions, all echelons, even the secondary echelon, must fully execute their tasks;

In relations with the masses, with the cadres, and with higher echelons, one must energetically oppose functionaire-ism and bureaucratism;

In the utilization of popular forces and of national property, one must absolutely oppose waste and bribery;

In the organization of forces and of popular initiative in the army and cadres, it is necessary to guide, to encourage and to follow in an efficient manner the popular and related movements.

The successes which we have realized during the last year in every field, as well as the international democratic and peace movement which supports our resistance, constitute the guarantee for our people, who may expect numerous additional successes for this year.

APPENDIX IV

SUMMARY GLOSSARY OF VIET-MINH ADMINISTRATIVE AND POLITICAL TERMS

This brief glossary does not pretend to be either complete or fully accurate, but it may help the English-language reader to understand certain terms and abbreviations which he may not find in a conventional Vietnamese dictionary, because many of them are recent transliterations of Chinese political terms.

Bac-Bo: North Vietnam; formerly Tongking.

Ban Can Su: Cadre Committee (mainly used in Cambodia).

Ban Chap Hanh Truong Uong: Central Executive Committee (Admin.).

Ban Giam Doc: Inspection Committee (mostly in armament).

Ban Giao Thong Lien Lac: Liaison and Communications Committee.

Ban Hoa Van Than Thien: Chinese Cultural and Friendship Committee

Ban Van Dong Thanh Lap Dong Dang Nhan Cach Mang Cao Mien: Canvassing Committee for the Creation of the Cambodian People's Revolutionary Party.

Bo Binh Phao: Artillery (Service).

Bo Tram Muu: General Staff.

Bo Quoc Fong Tong Tu-lenh: General Staff, Ministry of National Defense.

Can-bo: Cadre (generally detailed to local level as expert).

Chi-Bo: Branch or cell of DLD, unit at level over Tieu-to.

Chi Quan-Bao Thanh: Military Security Service (Branch).

Chinh Uy: Political Commissar.

Chu-luc: Main Force (i.e., Regular Army).

Cu'u Quoc: National Salvation (newspaper title and militia units).

Cong Binh: Engineers (Army).

Cong To Viet (C.T.V.): Public Prosecutor.

Dai-Doan Cong Phao: Heavy (Artillery and Engineers) Division.

Dai-Doan (DD): Division (etymologically "brigade"; but used as indicated).

Dai-Doi (dd): Company

Dan Quan: Militia

Dang Doan: Professional Inter-Group in DLD.

Dang Lao-Dong, or Viet-Nam Dang Lao-Dong, or DLD: Vietnam Workers' Party.

Dia-hat Quan: Guerilla groups (city) at ward level.

Dia-phuong Quan: Regional Troops.

Du-kich: Guerilla units.

Dich-van: Action Groups (used for "armed propaganda").

Dong Duong Cong San Dang, or DDCSD: Indochina Communist Party, or ICP.

Giam-doc Tu-phap: Director, Judicial Services.

Hiep-ly: Attorney (referring also to administrative assistants detailed to
     local administrations).

Hoi Cong-Giao Cu'u Quoc: Association of Catholics for National Salvation.

Hoi-dong Nhan-dan: Popular Assembly.

Hoi-dong Nhan-dan Xa: Village Popular Assembly.

Hoi Phat-Giao Cu'u Quoc: Buddhist Association for National Salvation.

Huyen: District.

Khu: Zone.

Lien-: United, Union, Inter-, etc.

Lien-Chi (LC): Inter-Branch.

Lien-Chi Chi-Bo (LC/CB): Directing Inter-Branch.

Lien-khu: Inter-zone.

Lien-lac Thong Tin: Signal Corps Liaison.

Lien-Viet: United National Front.

Minh-Huong: Sino-Vietnamese half-blood.

Nam-Bo: South Vietnam; formerly Cochinchina.

Ngan-hang Xuat-nhap Cang: Import-Export Bank.

Nha-que: Small farmer, peasant.

Phai Vien Lien-lac Chinh-Tri Tran va Dia-Phuong: Delegates for Political Liaison
     with Front and Interior (Viet-Minh civil administration in Laos).

Phao Binh: Artillery.

Phong Khong: Anti-Aircraft (weapons and units).

Quan Gioi: Ammunition Service (Army).

Quan Huan: Information and Education Service (Army).

Quan Bao: Military Intelligence.

Quan-Y: Military Medical Services.

Quoc Hoi: National Assembly.

Sip Song Chau T'ai: The 12 Thai Baronies (Thai area in Northwest Vietnam).

Srok, khum, phum: Cambodian provincial administrative units.

Su-Doan: Division (now obsolete -- see Dai-Doan -- and sometimes used for Brigade).

Tay-Bac: Northwest (Vietnam).

Tieu-Doan (td): Battalion (formerly used for Regiment).

Tieu-Doan Doc-lap: Independent Battalion (i.e., Battalion Combat Team).

Tieu-Doan Tap Trung Tinh (td-TTT): Provincial (i.e., semi-regular) battalion.

Tieu-to: Cell (basic party unit).

Tinh Doc Cu Si: Buddhist Association.

Toa-an Quan-Phap: Courts-Martial.

Toa-an Quan-Su: Military Tribunal.

Tong Chinh Uy: General Political Commissar.

Tong Chinh Bo; Tong-Bo: Central Executive Committee (DLD), i.e., Politburo.

Tong Cuc Cung Cap: Quartermaster Service.

Tong Tan-cong: General Counter-Offensive.

To Kiem Soat Thanh: City Control Cell (DLD).

Tro Chien: Escort, or Support (Guard or weapons).

Trung-Bo: Central Vietnam; formerly Annam.

Trung-Doan (TD): Regiment (formerly used as Brigade).

Uy Ban Hanh Chinh, or UBKC: Administrative Committee.

Uy Ban Khang Chien/Hanh Chinh, or UBKC/HC: Committee for Resistance and
    Administration (usual administrative unit).

Van Tai: Transport.

Ve Binh: Guard.

Viet-gian: Traitor to Vietnam.

Viet-Minh: see below.

Viet-Nam Cach Menh Dong Minh Hoi, or VNCMDMH: Vietnam Revolutionary League.

Viet-Nam Phuc Quoc Dang, or Phuc-Quoc: Vietnam Restoration Party.

Viet-Nam Doc-lap Dong Minh Hoi, or Viet-Minh (V.-M.): League for the Independence
    of Vietnam.

Viet-Nam Quoc Dan Dang, or VNQDD: Vietnam Nationalist Party.

SELECTED BIBLIOGRAPHY

1. English

Chinese World, daily newspaper, San Francisco, most issues.

Finkelstein, Lawrence S., American Policy in Southeast Asia, Institute of Pacific Relations, New York, 1951.

Foreign Broadcasting Intelligence Service, Daily Reports, Department of State, Washington, most issues.

Hammer, Ellen J., The Emergence of Vietnam, Institute of Pacific Relations, New York, 1947.

_____, The Struggle for Indochina, Stanford University Press, 1954.

Hsin Hua, New China News Agency, Press Reports, Peking and Hong Kong, most issues.

New Times, "Trud," weekly, Moscow, 1951-, various issues.

New York Times, 1945-1954, most issues.

Nguyen Duy Thanh, My four years with the Viet-Minh, Democratic Research Service, Bombay, 1950.

Rosinger, Lawrence K., and associates, The State of Asia, Knopf, New York, 1951.

Starobin, Joseph R., Eyewitness in Indo-China, Cameron & Kahn, New York, 1954.

Truong Chinh, The Democratic Republic of Viet-Nam is 7 Years Old, Rangoon, Burma, 1952.

V.A.F.A. Review, Bulletin of the Viet-Nam-American Friendship Association, Hanoi and New York, 1945-46.

Viet-Nam News, Weekly Bulletin of the Viet-Nam News Service, Rangoon, Burma, all issues since 1949.

2. French

Bulletin des Missions, St. André-lez-Bruges, Belgium, 1946 issues.

Celérier, Pierre (pseud.), Menaces sur le Viet-Nam, IDEO, Saigon, 1950.

Chassin, General G., La Conquête de la Chine par Mao-Tsé-Tung, Ed. Payot, Paris, 1951.

Climats (weekly), Paris, most issues.

Courtade, Pierre, La Rivière Noire, Les Editeurs Français Réunis, Paris, 1953.

142

Devillers, Philippe, Histoire du Viet-Nam, Ed. Seuil, Paris, 1952.

Despuech, Jacques, Le Trafic des Piastres, Ed. Deux Rives, Paris, 1953.

Dinfreville, Jacques (pseud.), L'Opération Indochine, Les Editions
    Inter-Nationales, Paris, 1953.

Goëldhieux, Claude, Quinze mois prisonnier chez les Viets, Ed. Juilliard,
    Paris, 1953.

Journal Français d'Extreme-Orient, daily, Saigon, most issues.

Journaux Officiels de la République Française, Assemblée Nationale, Conseil
    de la République, Conseil de l'Union Française, Paris, various issues.

Indochine Sudest Asiatique, monthly magazine, Saigon, most issues.

Le Monde, daily, Paris, various issues.

L'Union Française, daily, Saigon, most issues.

Marchand, Jean (General), Le Drame Indochinois, J. Peyronney et Cie, Paris,
    1953.

Mus, Paul, Viet-Nam- Sociologie d'une Guerre, Ed. du Seuil, Paris, 1952.

Partai Communiste Français, Le Monde du Socialisme et de la Paix, Documents
    Economiques du Comite Central, Paris, 1953.

Regards, weekly, Paris, special issue of January, 1952.

Sainteny, Jean, Histoire d'une Paix Manquée, Amiot-Dumont, Paris, 1953.

Vu Quoc Thong, La Décentralisation Administrative au Viêt-Nam, Presses
    Universitaires du Viêt-Nam, Hanoi, 1952.

Nguyen Ai Quoc (alias Ho Chi Minh), Le Procès de la Colonisation Française,
    Lib. du Travail, Paris, 1925.

Nguyen Tien Lang, Les Chemins de la Revolte, Amiot-Dumont, Paris, 1953.

Roy, Jules, La Bataille dans la Rizière, Gallimard, Paris, 1953.

Viet-Nam, Bi-weekly Bulletin of the Vietnamese High Commission in France,
    Paris, 1951-.

3. Vietnamese

Bo Luat Dien-dia (Land Reform Code), Vietnam National Government,
    Imprimerie des Journaux Officiels, Saigon, 1953.

Cu'u Quoc, daily, 1945-46 at Hanoi, now unknown location, printed in four
    regional editions.

Nhan-Dan, daily, publication of the Dang Lao-Dong, 1949-.

Viet-Nam, daily, Hanoi, 1945-46.

Viet-Nam Dan-Quoc Cong-Bao (Official Journal of the Democratic Republic),
Hanoi, 1945-46, then unknown location, printed intermittently in North
Vietnam.

4. Chinese

Chang Kuang-piao, From Colonialism to Independence in Indochina (No. 65
in the series "World Knowledge"), World Knowledge Press, Shanghai -
Peking, 1951.

Figueres, Leo, etc., The Liberation Movement of Indochina and the Aggression
of Imperialism, Ed. Sung Kuei-huang, Shanghai - Peking, 1951.

Jen-min ch'u-pan-she, Indochina in the Midst of her Struggle, New China
Press, Peking, 1951.

5. Other Sources

Akademia nauk SSSR, The National Liberation Struggle of the Peoples of
Eastern Asia, Tikho-okeanskii institut, Moscow, 1949. (Russian)

Halle, Guenther, Foreign Legion, Verlag Volk und Welt, East Berlin, 1952.
(German, Soviet Zone)

Muenchener Illustrierte, "And the fools get themselves killed" (an
anonymous serial in the September-October, 1953, issues), Munich, 1953.
(German)

Novoye vremia (New Times, Russian Edition, weekly), "Trud" Publishing
House, Moscow, various issues, particularly: October 1, 1947; April 23,
1948; August 8, 1950; September 8, 1950. (Russian)

Pravda (daily), Moscow, various issues, particularly: September 2, 19, 20,
21, 1953. (Russian)

U.S. Department of State, Ost-Probleme (weekly), U.S. High Commissioner
in Germany, Press Division, Bad Godesberg, Germany, 1950--, various
issues. (German)

NOTE: The titles of foreign sources other than French are given in their
approximate English translation.

Cornell University Southeast Asia Program

OFFICERS, FACULTY AND STAFF, 1953-54

Officers:

Deane W. Malott, President of the University
F. F. Hill, Provost of the University
S. S. Atwood, Dean of the Graduate School
Paul M. O'Leary, Dean of the College of Arts and Sciences
Knight Biggerstaff, Chairman of the Department of Far Eastern Studies

Faculty:

John M. Echols, Associate Professor of Linguistics
Lucien M. Hanks, Jr., Research Associate in Psychology and Field Director,
    Thailand Project (on leave from Bennington College)
Gussie E. Gaskill, Curator of the Wason Collection
Frank H. Golay, Assistant Professor of Economics
Charles F. Hockett, Professor of Linguistics
George McT. Kahin, Assistant Professor of Government and Associate Director
    of the Program
Lauriston Sharp, Professor of Anthropology and Director of the Program
G. William Skinner, Research Associate in Southeast Asian Studies and Field
    Director of the Program, Cornell Research Center, Bangkok
Charles Wolf, Jr., Visiting Professor of Economics and Southeast Asian Studies

Cooperating Faculty from Other Departments:

E. A. Burtt, Susan Linn Sage Professor of Philosophy
Hazel M. Hauck, Professor of Foods and Nutrition
Edward H. Litchfield, Dean, School of Business and Public Administration
F. G. Marcham, Goldwin Smith Professor of History
Robert A. Polson, Professor of Rural Sociology

Staff:

Samiati Alisjahbana, Teaching Assistant in Indonesian
Bernard B. Fall, Research Assistant in the Program
Alejandro M. Fernandez, Research Assistant in the Program
William W. Gage, Teaching Assistant in Vietnamese
Jane R. Hanks, Research Associate in Anthropology and Associate Field Director,
    Thailand Project
Claire Holt, Research Associate in Southeast Asian Studies and Field Director,
    Indonesian Arts Project
Kamol Janlekha, Research Assistant in the Program
James T. Peng, Research Consultant, Cornell Research Center, Bangkok
Cynthia J. Wellenkamp, Secretary to the Program

DATA PAPERS

Number 1. REPORT ON THE CHINESE IN SOUTHEAST ASIA, DECEMBER 1950, by G. William Skinner, February 1951. (Supply exhausted)

Number 2. A CENTRAL JAVANESE VILLAGE IN 1950, by Paul M. Kattenburg, June 1951. (Supply exhausted)

Number 3. AN ACCOUNT OF AN ACQUISITION TRIP IN THE COUNTRIES OF SOUTHEAST ASIA, by Cecil Hobbs, February 1952. (Supply exhausted)

Number 4. THAI CULTURE AND BEHAVIOR, An Unpublished War Time Study Dated September 1943, by Ruth Benedict, February 1952. (Supply exhausted)

Number 5. RURAL ORGANIZATION AND VILLAGE REVIVAL IN INDONESIA, by Ch. J. Grader, April 1952. (Supply exhausted)

Number 6. TEACHING AND RESEARCH RELATING TO SOUTHEAST ASIA IN AMERICAN COLLEGES AND UNIVERSITIES, APRIL 1952, by George McT. Kahin, September 1952. (Supply exhausted)

Number 7. LABOUR AND TIN MINING IN MALAYA, by Nim Chee Siew, February 1953.

Number 8. SURVEY OF CHINESE LANGUAGE MATERIALS ON SOUTHEAST ASIA IN THE HOOVER INSTITUTE AND LIBRARY, by Giok Po Oey, May 1953.

Number 9. VERB CONSTRUCTIONS IN VIETNAMESE, by William W. Gage and H. Merrill Jackson, July 1953.

Number 10. AN ACCOUNT OF THE JAPANESE OCCUPATION OF BANJUMAS RESIDENCY, JAVA, MARCH 1942 TO AUGUST 1945, by S. M. Gandasubrata, Resident of Banjumas, August 1953.

Number 11. ACCOUNT OF A TRIP TO THE COUNTRIES OF SOUTHEAST ASIA FOR THE LIBRARY OF CONGRESS, 1952-1953, by Cecil Hobbs, December 1953.

Number 12. POLITICAL INSTITUTIONS OF OLD BURMA, by John F. Cady, April 1954.

Number 13. TADAGALE: A BURMESE VILLAGE IN 1950, by Charles S. Brant, April 1954.

Number 14. THE VIET-MINH REGIME: GOVERNMENT AND ADMINISTRATION IN THE DEMOCRATIC REPULBIC OF VIETNAM, by Bernard B. Fall, April, 1954. (Issued jointly with the Institute of Pacific Relations, 1 East 54th Street, New York 22, New York.)

Representative Thai Musical Instruments

Performed or directed by Kamon Ketusiri, recorded and narrated by Carol Skinner, in Thailand. Two 12-inch long playing records (4 sides). $10.00.

6927 002